KEMAL ATATÜRK

KEMAL ATATÜRK

Frank Tachau

CHELSEA HOUSE PUBLISHERS
NEW YORK
PHILADELPHIA

EDITOR-IN-CHIEF: Nancy Toff
EXECUTIVE EDITOR: Remmel T. Nunn
MANAGING EDITOR: Karyn Gullen Browne
COPY CHIEF: Juliann Barbato
ART DIRECTOR: Giannella Garrett
MANUFACTURING MANAGER: Gerald Levine

Staff for KEMAL ATATÜRK:

SENIOR EDITOR: John W. Selfridge
ASSISTANT EDITORS: Maria Behan, Pierre Hauser, Kathleen McDermott, Bert Yaeger
EDITORIAL ASSISTANT: James Guiry
COPY EDITORS: Gillian Bucky, Sean Dolan, Ellen Scordato
PICTURE EDITOR: Juliette Dickstein
DESIGN ASSISTANT: Jill Goldreyer
PICTURE RESEARCH: Toby Greenberg
LAYOUT: David Murray
PRODUCTION COORDINATOR: Laura McCormick
COVER ILLUSTRATION: Lisa Young

CREATIVE DIRECTOR: Harold Steinberg

Frontispiece courtesy of Turkish Culture and Information Office, N.Y.

3 5 7 9 8 6 4 2

Library of Congress Cataloging in Publication Data

Tachau, Frank . KEMAL ATATÜRK

(World leaders past & present)
Bibliography: p.
Includes index.
1. Atatürk, Kemal, 1881–1938. 2. Turkey—Presidents—
Biography. I. Title. II. Series: World leaders past & present.
DR592.K4T25   1987   956.1′024′0924 [B]   87-6635

ISBN 0-87754-507-3
     0-7910-0612-3 (pbk.)

Contents

ADENAUER	FREDERICK THE GREAT	MARY, QUEEN OF SCOTS
ALEXANDER THE GREAT	INDIRA GANDHI	GOLDA MEIR
MARC ANTONY	MOHANDAS GANDHI	METTERNICH
KING ARTHUR	GARIBALDI	MUSSOLINI
ATATÜRK	GENGHIS KHAN	NAPOLEON
ATTLEE	GLADSTONE	NASSER
BEGIN	GORBACHEV	NEHRU
BEN-GURION	HAMMARSKJÖLD	NERO
BISMARCK	HENRY VIII	NICHOLAS II
LÉON BLUM	HENRY OF NAVARRE	NIXON
BOLÍVAR	HINDENBURG	NKRUMAH
CESARE BORGIA	HITLER	PERICLES
BRANDT	HO CHI MINH	PERÓN
BREZHNEV	HUSSEIN	QADDAFI
CAESAR	IVAN THE TERRIBLE	ROBESPIERRE
CALVIN	ANDREW JACKSON	ELEANOR ROOSEVELT
CASTRO	JEFFERSON	FRANKLIN D. ROOSEVELT
CATHERINE THE GREAT	JOAN OF ARC	THEODORE ROOSEVELT
CHARLEMAGNE	POPE JOHN XXIII	SADAT
CHIANG KAI-SHEK	LYNDON JOHNSON	STALIN
CHURCHILL	JUÁREZ	SUN YAT-SEN
CLEMENCEAU	JOHN F. KENNEDY	TAMERLANE
CLEOPATRA	KENYATTA	THATCHER
CORTÉS	KHOMEINI	TITO
CROMWELL	KHRUSHCHEV	TROTSKY
DANTON	MARTIN LUTHER KING, JR.	TRUDEAU
DE GAULLE	KISSINGER	TRUMAN
DE VALERA	LENIN	VICTORIA
DISRAELI	LINCOLN	WASHINGTON
EISENHOWER	LLOYD GEORGE	WEIZMANN
ELEANOR OF AQUITAINE	LOUIS XIV	WOODROW WILSON
QUEEN ELIZABETH I	LUTHER	XERXES
FERDINAND AND ISABELLA	JUDAS MACCABEUS	ZHOU ENLAI
FRANCO	MAO ZEDONG	

ON LEADERSHIP
Arthur M. Schlesinger, jr.

LEADERSHIP, it may be said, is really what makes the world go round. Love no doubt smooths the passage; but love is a private transaction between consenting adults. Leadership is a public transaction with history. The idea of leadership affirms the capacity of individuals to move, inspire, and mobilize masses of people so that they act together in pursuit of an end. Sometimes leadership serves good purposes, sometimes bad; but whether the end is benign or evil, great leaders are those men and women who leave their personal stamp on history.

Now, the very concept of leadership implies the proposition that individuals can make a difference. This proposition has never been universally accepted. From classical times to the present day, eminent thinkers have regarded individuals as no more than the agents and pawns of larger forces, whether the gods and goddesses of the ancient world or, in the modern era, race, class, nation, the dialectic, the will of the people, the spirit of the times, history itself. Against such forces, the individual dwindles into insignificance.

So contends the thesis of historical determinism. Tolstoy's great novel *War and Peace* offers a famous statement of the case. Why, Tolstoy asked, did millions of men in the Napoleonic wars, denying their human feelings and their common sense, move back and forth across Europe slaughtering their fellows? "The war," Tolstoy answered, "was bound to happen simply because it was bound to happen." All prior history predetermined it. As for leaders, they, Tolstoy said, "are but the labels that serve to give a name to an end and, like labels, they have the least possible connection with the event." The greater the leader, "the more conspicuous the inevitability and the predestination of every act he commits." The leader, said Tolstoy, is "the slave of history."

Determinism takes many forms. Marxism is the determinism of class. Nazism the determinism of race. But the idea of men and women as the slaves of history runs athwart the deepest human instincts. Rigid determinism abolishes the idea of human freedom—

the assumption of free choice that underlies every move we make, every word we speak, every thought we think. It abolishes the idea of human responsibility, since it is manifestly unfair to reward or punish people for actions that are by definition beyond their control. No one can live consistently by any deterministic creed. The Marxist states prove this themselves by their extreme susceptibility to the cult of leadership.

More than that, history refutes the idea that individuals make no difference. In December 1931 a British politician crossing Park Avenue in New York City between 76th and 77th Streets around 10:30 P.M. looked in the wrong direction and was knocked down by an automobile—a moment, he later recalled, of a man aghast, a world aglare: "I do not understand why I was not broken like an eggshell or squashed like a gooseberry." Fourteen months later an American politician, sitting in an open car in Miami, Florida, was fired on by an assassin; the man beside him was hit. Those who believe that individuals make no difference to history might well ponder whether the next two decades would have been the same had Mario Constasino's car killed Winston Churchill in 1931 and Giuseppe Zangara's bullet killed Franklin Roosevelt in 1933. Suppose, in addition, that Adolf Hitler had been killed in the street fighting during the Munich *Putsch* of 1923 and that Lenin had died of typhus during World War I. What would the 20th century be like now?

For better or for worse, individuals do make a difference. "The notion that a people can run itself and its affairs anonymously," wrote the philosopher William James, "is now well known to be the silliest of absurdities. Mankind does nothing save through initiatives on the part of inventors, great or small, and imitation by the rest of us—these are the sole factors in human progress. Individuals of genius show the way, and set the patterns, which common people then adopt and follow."

Leadership, James suggests, means leadership in thought as well as in action. In the long run, leaders in thought may well make the greater difference to the world. But, as Woodrow Wilson once said, "Those only are leaders of men, in the general eye, who lead in action. . . . It is at their hands that new thought gets its translation into the crude language of deeds." Leaders in thought often invent in solitude and obscurity, leaving to later generations the tasks of imitation. Leaders in action—the leaders portrayed in this series—have to be effective in their own time.

And they cannot be effective by themselves. They must act in response to the rhythms of their age. Their genius must be adapted, in a phrase of William James's, "to the receptivities of the moment." Leaders are useless without followers. "There goes the mob," said the French politician hearing a clamor in the streets. "I am their leader. I must follow them." Great leaders turn the inchoate emotions of the mob to purposes of their own. They seize on the opportunities of their time, the hopes, fears, frustrations, crises, potentialities. They succeed when events have prepared the way for them, when the community is awaiting to be aroused, when they can provide the clarifying and organizing ideas. Leadership ignites the circuit between the individual and the mass and thereby alters history.

It may alter history for better or for worse. Leaders have been responsible for the most extravagant follies and most monstrous crimes that have beset suffering humanity. They have also been vital in such gains as humanity has made in individual freedom, religious and racial tolerance, social justice and respect for human rights.

There is no sure way to tell in advance who is going to lead for good and who for evil. But a glance at the gallery of men and women in *World Leaders—Past and Present* suggests some useful tests.

One test is this: do leaders lead by force or by persuasion? By command or by consent? Through most of history leadership was exercised by the divine right of authority. The duty of followers was to defer and to obey. "Theirs not to reason why,/ Theirs but to do and die." On occasion, as with the so-called "enlightened despots" of the 18th century in Europe, absolutist leadership was animated by humane purposes. More often, absolutism nourished the passion for domination, land, gold and conquest and resulted in tyranny.

The great revolution of modern times has been the revolution of equality. The idea that all people should be equal in their legal condition has undermined the old structure of authority, hierarchy and deference. The revolution of equality has had two contrary effects on the nature of leadership. For equality, as Alexis de Tocqueville pointed out in his great study *Democracy in America,* might mean equality in servitude as well as equality in freedom.

"I know of only two methods of establishing equality in the political world," Tocqueville wrote. "Rights must be given to every citizen, or none at all to anyone . . . save one, who is the master of all." There was no middle ground "between the sovereignty of all and the absolute power of one man." In his astonishing prediction of 20th-century totalitarian dictatorship, Tocqueville explained how the revolution of equality could lead to the *"Führerprinzip"* and more terrible absolutism than the world had ever known.

But when rights are given to every citizen and the sovereignty of all is established, the problem of leadership takes a new form, becomes more exacting than ever before. It is easy to issue commands and enforce them by the rope and the stake, the concentration camp and the *gulag*. It is much harder to use argument and achievement to overcome opposition and win consent. The Founding Fathers of the United States understood the difficulty. They believed that history had given them the opportunity to decide, as Alexander Hamilton wrote in the first Federalist Paper, whether men are indeed capable of basing government on "reflection and choice, or whether they are forever destined to depend . . . on accident and force."

Government by reflection and choice called for a new style of leadership and a new quality of followership. It required leaders to be responsive to popular concerns, and it required followers to be active and informed participants in the process. Democracy does not eliminate emotion from politics; sometimes it fosters demagoguery; but it is confident that, as the greatest of democratic leaders put it, you cannot fool all of the people all of the time. It measures leadership by results and retires those who overreach or falter or fail.

It is true that in the long run despots are measured by results too. But they can postpone the day of judgment, sometimes indefinitely, and in the meantime they can do infinite harm. It is also true that democracy is no guarantee of virtue and intelligence in government, for the voice of the people is not necessarily the voice of God. But democracy, by assuring the right of opposition, offers built-in resistance to the evils inherent in absolutism. As the theologian Reinhold Niebuhr summed it up, "Man's capacity for justice makes democracy possible, but man's inclination to injustice makes democracy necessary."

A second test for leadership is the end for which power is sought. When leaders have as their goal the supremacy of a master race or the promotion of totalitarian revolution or the acquisition and exploitation of colonies or the protection of greed and privilege or the preservation of personal power, it is likely that their leadership will do little to advance the cause of humanity. When their goal is the abolition of slavery, the liberation of women, the enlargement of opportunity for the poor and powerless, the extension of equal rights to racial minorities, the defense of the freedoms of expression and opposition, it is likely that their leadership will increase the sum of human liberty and welfare.

Leaders have done great harm to the world. They have also conferred great benefits. You will find both sorts in this series. Even "good" leaders must be regarded with a certain wariness. Leaders are not demigods; they put on their trousers one leg after another just like ordinary mortals. No leader is infallible, and every leader needs to be reminded of this at regular intervals. Irreverence irritates leaders but is their salvation. Unquestioning submission corrupts leaders and demands followers. Making a cult of a leader is always a mistake. Fortunately hero worship generates its own antidote. "Every hero," said Emerson, "becomes a bore at last."

The signal benefit the great leaders confer is to embolden the rest of us to live according to our own best selves, to be active, insistent, and resolute in affirming our own sense of things. For great leaders attest to the reality of human freedom against the supposed inevitabilities of history. And they attest to the wisdom and power that may lie within the most unlikely of us, which is why Abraham Lincoln remains the supreme example of great leadership. A great leader, said Emerson, exhibits new possibilities to all humanity. "We feed on genius. . . . Great men exist that there may be greater men."

Great leaders, in short, justify themselves by emancipating and empowering their followers. So humanity struggles to master its destiny, remembering with Alexis de Tocqueville: "It is true that around every man a fatal circle is traced beyond which he cannot pass; but within the wide verge of that circle he is powerful and free; as it is with man, so with communities."

1

The Hero of Gallipoli

Lieutenant Colonel Mustafa Kemal, division commander in the Ottoman army, was in the process of marching his men to the battlefront in what was to be one of the decisive battles of World War I. The scene was a rugged peninsula in Turkey called Gallipoli, where poorly equipped Ottoman Turkish soldiers were trying to defend their country against invasion by the British.

The stakes were extremely high. The British were attempting to use Gallipoli as a foothold in order to capture nearby Istanbul, the capital of the Ottoman Empire. This would allow them to use the Black Sea to send badly needed supplies to their Russian allies, who were being beaten by Turkey's allies, the Germans. Such an English victory would probably mean the end of Turkish independence — and to Mustafa Kemal, that would be catastrophic. Kemal was an ardent nationalist who was determined to defend his country, whatever the cost.

Great Britain was an immensely powerful enemy. As dawn broke on April 25, 1915, Britain used part of its vast naval fleet to land thousands of troops on the Gallipoli beaches. Most of these troops were from Australia and New Zealand, which were part of the British Empire at that time.

> *When its independence is in danger, the nation recruits its own armies and adopts but one attitude: to sacrifice its blood to the last for its own salvation.*
> —MUSTAFA KEMAL

Mustafa Kemal was adept at inspiring loyalty in the soldiers under his command. After the Battle of Gallipoli, his bravery and leadership skills became legendary.

TURKISH CULTURE AND INFORMATION OFFICE, N.Y.

During World War I, the city of Istanbul became the target of Allied invaders. The British hoped to capture the ancient Ottoman capital after landing on the nearby Gallipoli peninsula.

Compared to the considerable resources commanded by the British forces, Turkey was at a great disadvantage. Supplies were low, and morale was slipping. The several thousand men under Kemal's command badly needed rest, and so the young officer ordered that they stop for a time while he went on ahead. Soon he ran directly into two Turkish scouts who were fleeing in panic from the enemy.

Kemal stopped them and asked, "Why are you running away?"

"They come! They come!" the men shouted, their eyes wide with fear.

"Who comes?"

"Sir, the enemy! The English! The English!"

Kemal looked in the direction the men were pointing and saw Australian soldiers advancing without any opposition.

"You cannot run away," he told the men sternly.

"But our ammunition is finished!" they protested.

"You have your bayonets," he replied and ordered the Turks to fix bayonets and fall to the ground. Then Kemal sent a messenger to tell his own infantrymen to get there on the double.

When the British soldiers saw their fleeing adversaries preparing to fight again, they hesitated. This gave Mustafa Kemal time to gather reinforcements and to counterattack. He and his men plunged into the battle. Kemal directed his troops on horseback, riding up to the front lines in complete disregard for his own safety. In his determination to forestall the invasion, he had told his men, "I don't order you to attack, I order you to die. In the time it takes us to die, other troops and commanders can come and take our place."

British troops land on the shores of Gallipoli on April 25, 1915. A far-sighted strategist, Mustafa Kemal had suspected that the Allies might stage an attack here in order to open military supply routes on the Black Sea.

Kemal had not underestimated the number of lives the Battle of Gallipoli would claim that day. Entire Turkish regiments were cut down by enemy rifle fire, but, spurred by their seemingly fearless commander, the Ottoman army had driven Great Britain's forces back toward the coast.

Even after nightfall, the fighting continued. As one historian later wrote, there was "no rest for anyone on those rugged hillsides that night. Worn out with fatigue, scattered and disorganized, it was impossible for either side to make further progress. But the noise of battle continued; and with only the flash of their assailants' rifles to guide them, invaders and invaded alike kept up a continuous fire."

Stunned by the fierce tenacity of the Turkish resistance, the commander of the British forces at Gallipoli sent word to his commander in chief that his forces had been defeated and asked permission to evacuate. His request was denied, and the fighting raged for weeks while casualties mounted on both sides. Thanks in no small part to the military skill of Mustafa Kemal, the Turks finally won the battle.

Ottoman soldiers prepare their guns before facing the enemy on the rugged battlefields of Gallipoli. Although the British forces had more sophisticated arms at their disposal, Kemal's troops prevented their enemies from making inroads into Ottoman territory.

THE BETTMANN ARCHIVE

The Battle of Gallipoli enhanced Kemal's reputation for loyalty, bravery, and brilliant leadership. In spite of this victory, however, the war ended with the thorough defeat of Turkey. Although Mustafa Kemal had had many ideas that he thought might have prevented this outcome, he had been unable to persuade his country's senior military commanders and government leaders to listen.

But Kemal would soon learn to make his countrymen listen. In the chaos and disorder that followed the war, Mustafa Kemal would save his nation from disaster.

Although Kemal initially had to convince fearful Ottoman scouts to stand and fight their seemingly invincible British adversaries, the Ottoman army performed heroically during the bloody Battle of Gallipoli.

2

The Pride of Youth

Mustafa was born in 1881 in the city of Salonika in the Ottoman Empire. Instead of the black hair and dark eyes so typical of his people, Mustafa had sandy hair, blue eyes, and light skin. From the beginning, his distinctive appearance set him apart.

Even at a very young age Mustafa had ideas of his own that he often insisted on carrying out, despite the objections of his parents, Ali Riza and his wife Zübeyde. He was a special child in their eyes, particularly because three of their children had died in infancy, with only Mustafa and his sister, Makbule, surviving. Mustafa's mother and father often gave in to his persistence and determination, and he must have learned early on that these qualities could pay off. The loss of his father, a customs officer turned businessman, when Mustafa was only seven probably also helped bring out the boy's independent, strong will.

The Ottoman Empire of Mustafa's youth was huge, but in a state of decline. In the 13th century Sultan Osman had founded the Ottoman dynasty in Anatolia, the western area of Asia also known as Asia Minor. The Ottoman rulers had quickly expanded their influence, and the empire reached its height in the 16th century. During the course of

The day will come when I shall have realized all the reforms which today you consider as dreams. The nation to which I belong will believe in me.
—MUSTAFA KEMAL
1907

Mustafa Kemal, who took the name Atatürk (Father Turk) in 1934, was a proud and driven individual. Even during his childhood, his serious nature set him apart from his contemporaries.

Sultan Osman, the 13th-century founder of the Ottoman Empire, announces his acceptance of the Muslim faith. Traditionally, religious and governmental authority were linked in the empire — the sultan also served as his people's spiritual leader.

the next 300 years Turkish armies were defeated in many wars, and much territory was lost, especially to the Russians. The empire was also threatened by tensions that ran high among the various ethnic groups that had come under Turkish rule. At the time of Mustafa's youth the Ottoman Empire included people of many different nationalities, and its boundaries ran from the heart of Europe bordering the Austro-Hungarian Empire to the shores of the Black Sea and south to the Arabian Peninsula. It included parts or all of present-day Cyprus, Yugoslavia, Romania, Bulgaria, Albania, Greece, Iraq, Syria, Libya, Yemen, Southern Yemen, Lebanon, and Saudi Arabia.

Most citizens of Salonika, Mustafa's birthplace, were not Turks at all, but Greek, Albanian, Jewish, or Bulgarian. Mustafa thus grew up with an awareness of the differences among the many types of people living in the empire, differences that were heightened when the various peoples in the empire fought for their political independence — against each other and particularly against the Turks.

Young Mustafa quickly grew to understand what it meant to be a Turk and a member of a minority group that ruled all others within the empire. Because Salonika was a large port city, Mustafa also became familiar with foreigners, especially Europeans, who were engaged in business and trade. He admired their wealth and power, and their skill in business, science, and technology.

After Mustafa's father died, Zübeyde, who wanted her son to become a Muslim preacher, enrolled him in a religious school. He rebelled, however, and over the next few years rejected one school after another, claiming that he did not like the clothes he was required to wear or that he could not get along with his teachers, some of whom beat him because of his rebelliousness.

Finally, when he was 12, Mustafa decided that he wanted to go to military school. He had always been impressed with the Turkish soldiers who paraded in their fancy uniforms through the streets crowded with foreigners — and with the way that everyone respectfully made room for them.

> *Stealthily the West was creeping in, trying to lure the East with her wonders. . . . But vaguely we sensed the coldness of her glitter and the price of her wooing.*
>
> —a Turkish contemporary on Salonika in the 1890s

A Muslim mosque dominates this typical Anatolian landscape. Although the Ottoman Empire encompassed territories in Europe and Asia, its heartland lay in Anatolia, or Asia Minor, the home of the ethnic Turks.

Yugoslavians were one of the numerous ethnic groups that came under Ottoman domination during the empire's long history. Growing up in the cosmopolitan city of Salonika, Mustafa soon became aware of the fact that Turks were a minority within their own empire.

Although his mother at first refused to permit him to enroll in Salonika's Military Secondary School, Mustafa, who had secretly taken and passed the entrance examination, was insistent. He reminded her that his father had given him a sword at birth, a sign that he wanted his only son to join the military. "I was born as a soldier," he told her dramatically, "I shall die as a soldier."

Mustafa's personality was well suited to military school. A loner with few friends, he had always been too proud and reserved to participate in games with his peers. As a small child, he had claimed that bending over to play leapfrog was undignified and had challenged the other children to jump over him while he stood upright. In his new high school, however, he found opportunities not only to acquire the proud bearing of a soldier but also to show off his exceptional intelligence.

Mathematics was his favorite subject, and he quickly developed a special relationship with the teacher. Following Turkish custom, the teacher rewarded his favorite gifted student with a great compliment: a second name. The new name, "Kemal," is the Turkish word for "perfection." This talented, intelligent, and rather vain boy accepted the name eagerly, and was from then on known either as Mustafa Kemal, or simply as Kemal.

Kemal finished military preparatory school in two years. In 1895, at the age of 14, he was admitted to the Military Training School in Monastir, in what is today Yugoslavia. The four years he spent at school in Monastir were very important in his development. The region was filled with unrest, and whenever trouble broke out, tensions were felt in the school, where members of student political factions often fought one another. Although Kemal shrewdly avoided these fights, he maneuvered behind the scenes to become the leader of the cadets from Salonika. He began to feel intensely patriotic toward the Ottoman Turkish Empire and deeply loyal to his fellow Turks. In 1897 Greek rebels tried to free the island of Crete from Turkish rule, and Kemal ran away to volunteer for the Ottoman army. He was bitterly disappointed when he was recognized as a student from the training school and thereupon returned.

Mustafa Kemal was also deeply affected by the new ideas he encountered at school. He learned French and began reading some of the great French liberal political philosophers, such as Jean-Jacques Rousseau, Voltaire, and Montesquieu. He and his fellow cadets would argue among themselves about how these ideas could be applied to bring about badly needed reform in the Ottoman social and political system. Kemal formed lifelong friendships with many of his classmates, and some became close political associates later on.

The sultan of the Ottoman Empire, Abdülhamid II, sponsored some minor reforms in the government but was completely opposed to the sweeping sort of reform for which Kemal and his friends

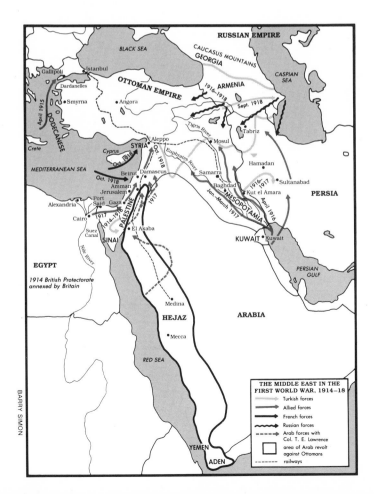

The Ottoman Empire c. 1895, the year Kemal entered the Military Training School in Monastir. During his lifetime, Kemal saw this vast empire shrink — Monastir eventually became part of Yugoslavia, and even Salonika, his birthplace, came under foreign rule.

BARRY SIMON

THE MIDDLE EAST IN THE
FIRST WORLD WAR, 1914–18

- Turkish forces
- Allied forces
- French forces
- Russian forces
- Arab forces with Col. T. E. Lawrence
- area of Arab revolt against Ottomans
- railways

Greek troops scale a mountainside during the offensive that began the 1897 war between the Greeks and the Turks. Although the 16-year-old Kemal was turned away when he tried to join the Ottoman army in this conflict, he would fight—and defeat—the Greek army when he reached maturity.

longed. His goal was to preserve the Ottoman sultanate and to suppress any movement toward democracy. Advocating liberal political ideas was absolutely forbidden in the empire — whether in the form of organized political activity or in writing. Offenders were thrown in prison or exiled to remote corners of the empire. Few returned alive.

Although the cadets were limited in what they could read or even discuss openly, Mustafa Kemal's life was not completely restricted. Back in Salonika during vacations, he enjoyed the free and easy social life of the cafés near the waterfront. He quickly discovered drinking, dancing, and talking with women — all strictly forbidden in the traditional Muslim society into which he was born. Women found Kemal quite attractive, and he was very popular.

Neither his explorations of political philosophy nor his active social life affected his schoolwork. In 1899, when Kemal was 18, he was admitted to the elite War College of the Ottoman army in Istanbul. Kemal secretly continued to read about such liberal ideas as equal rights for all citizens and the need for governments to represent all individuals, rather than only a privileged few. At the age of 21 the high-spirited, supremely self-confident Turk graduated as a lieutenant, with the admirable ranking of eighth in a graduating class of 459.

In recognition of his superb scholastic performance, Lieutenant Mustafa Kemal was then admitted to the highly select Staff College. Yet the young officer was often depressed and unable to sleep. He was upset not only by the repressive political conditions of his time, but also by his feeling that being among the very best just was not enough. He wanted to become a recognized leader, within the army and throughout the empire.

As time went on Kemal's depression and frustration led him to engage in increasingly dangerous political activities. After graduating from the Staff College at the age of 24, Kemal, who was now a captain, rented an apartment in Istanbul with a group of friends, including a former classmate, Ali Fuad. They assumed that they could safely hold discussions there without interference from the authorities, but one among them was a spy who informed the government of their activities. Kemal was imprisoned and interrogated relentlessly. At the very least his commission as an army officer was in jeopardy; at worst he might be sentenced to a long prison term.

Thus it was that just as the young Turk concluded his years of professional study and training — just as he stood at the threshold of what might become a brilliant military career — his entire future was threatened.

3

The Young Turks

The punishment chosen for Mustafa Kemal after his arrest and interrogation could not have been better designed to make him miserable. Along with his close friend Ali Fuad and another classmate, he was exiled from the lively life of Istanbul and assigned to the Fifth Army, which was based in the isolated city of Damascus, Syria, then part of the Ottoman Empire. In the early 20th century no direct railroad or highway connected the two cities, and several mountain ranges lay between them. Damascus itself was shrouded in traditional Muslim customs and offered none of the social activities of Salonika and Istanbul. Furthermore, Kemal's fellow officers in Damascus knew that he and his friends were in exile, and they were suspicious and unfriendly.

To make matters still worse, the Fifth Army was highly undisciplined and corrupt. The soldiers spent most of their time controlling quarrels among local villagers and townspeople. Many took advantage of these missions to extort money from the people they were supposed to protect; if the people resisted, the Ottoman officers and soldiers simply looted their houses.

Many are the youth of this country who are willing to sacrifice their own safety and happiness for that of their nation.
—MUSTAFA KEMAL
1912

An Arab stares out into the desert that surrounds this Muslim monastery in North Africa. After Kemal's exile to Damascus, Syria, he tried to enlist the Arab population in his revolutionary Fatherland Society, but language and cultural barriers prevented the European-oriented idealist from attracting many followers.

THE BETTMANN ARCHIVE

In 1906 Kemal's disgust with this state of affairs drove him to help in the formation of a revolutionary political society called *Vatan*, the "Fatherland Society." He wanted to do away with social and intellectual repression as well as the corruption in the government and army — in other words, to make the Ottoman Empire democratic. But Kemal was young and lacking in experience; he was able to attract only a few fellow Turkish officers. The local Arabs spoke a different language, and, because they were unfamiliar with European languages and ideas, they had few complaints about their situation.

A page from the Koran, the holy text of Islam. Many Turks lived their lives in accordance with the Koran's teachings — a practice that Kemal would eventually discourage.

THE BETTMANN ARCHIVE

The Christian peoples under Ottoman rule, such as this Serbian peasant woman, frequently proved to be unruly subjects of the Muslim Ottoman government. This volatile political situation enabled a group of reform-minded young soldiers — the Young Turks — to force concessions from Sultan Abdulhamid.

In frustration, Kemal wrote to an Ottoman general in Salonika asking for help with his radical group. Misreading the general's cool response, Kemal persuaded some fellow officers to cover for him while he sneaked back to Salonika to find the man who supposedly would aid him. Though the general refused to help him, Kemal stayed in his native city for several months and managed to establish a tiny branch of his brand-new revolutionary society.

Kemal found Salonika very much changed. Unrest among the empire's Christian peoples, especially the Bulgarians, Greeks, and Macedonians, had vastly increased. The great powers of Europe had sent undercover agents into the area to try to take advantage of the growing disorder. In turn, Sultan Abdülhamid had sent thousands of his own agents to try to turn the various factions against one another to weaken their opposition to his government. Patriotic Turks were in despair: their country was seemingly being torn apart by rebellious Christians, foreign interests, and the repressive power of their own government.

The Ottoman Parliament, which Sultan Abdülhamid had stubbornly refused to convene for over 30 years, reopened on December 17, 1908, several months after the Young Turk Revolution.

In the early 20th century some Turkish exiles who opposed Abdülhamid's policies formed a group that came to be known as the Young Turks. The movement spread throughout the empire and was eventually taken over by a group of army officers who called themselves the Committee of Union and Progress (CUP). These youthful idealists fought both the disruptive minorities and the dictatorial government. Events came to a head when the sultan's agents shot and killed one of the Young Turks.

Feeling cornered, the young officers fled to the hills along with some soldiers and declared open rebellion against the sultan. They demanded that he restore the Constitution of 1876, which provided for a parliamentary government — one in which the interests of the people would be represented. The sultan sent reinforcements to overcome the rebellion, but they joined the rebels instead. Finally Sultan Abdülhamid gave in to the rebels. On July 24, 1908, he issued a declaration restoring the constitution and reconvening the parliament that he had adjourned more than 30 years before.

This momentous event, known as the Young Turk Revolution, marked the beginning of rapid political change in the Ottoman Empire. It unleashed a tremendous wave of public enthusiasm and hopefulness. Muslims, Christians, and Jews walked arm in arm, according to one historian. Turkish women dropped their traditional veils, jail gates were thrown open, political prisoners freed. Democracy was on everyone's mind.

Although Kemal supported the Young Turks, he disliked their leader, a young officer named Enver. In many ways he was like Kemal: energetic, tireless, and vain. Unlike Kemal, however, he was a religious man, and he neither smoked nor drank. Kemal thought the officer was a good soldier but feared he would never make a good political leader. He also envied Enver's popularity, and Enver's supporters decided Kemal was dangerous. They arranged to have him reassigned to a remote army unit at Tripoli, Libya, which was then part of the Ottoman Empire.

Naturally I'm jealous of him.
—MUSTAFA KEMAL
on Enver after the Young
Turk Revolution

Enver, the leader of the Young Turks, won a place in the Ottoman government — and the envy of Mustafa Kemal — after his followers succeeded in weakening the sultan. Threatened by Kemal's ambitions, Enver did his best to deprive him of widespread recognition.

Libya proved to be a tough testing ground. Local Arab tribes and religious sheikhs were even harder to control there than in Syria. In nearly open rebellion against the Ottoman government, these Arabs had imprisoned the Turkish officers who had preceded Kemal. Plunging into his difficult work with zest, Kemal asserted his authority as a representative of the CUP over the Turkish commander and his troops. Then he won over the Arab rebels by telling them that the new government in Istanbul would hear their complaints and provide protection.

Kemal next turned his attentions to the sheikh of Benghazi, a wily and difficult man. He intimidated the sheikh by surrounding his house with Turkish troops. He then promised that no harm would befall the caliph, religious leader of all Libyan Muslims, if the sheikh would recognize the authority of the new Turkish government. Faced with Turkish guns, the sheikh agreed.

Proud of these successes, Kemal returned to Salonika only to find that the Young Turk regime was in danger. While Abdülhamid battled the Young Turks, the Bulgarians had declared their independence from Turkish rule, Austria had seized the

The triumphant Young Turks parade through the streets of Istanbul after forcing Sultan Abdülhamid from his throne in 1909. As chief of staff of the army that marched on the capital, Kemal had a hand in the victory.

BROWN BROTHERS

Sultan Mehmed V became the puppet ruler of the Ottoman Empire following the deposition of his brother. The real power lay with Enver and the Young Turks.

provinces of Bosnia and Herzegovina, and the people of the island of Crete voted to unite with mainland Greece. In the capital city of Istanbul, religious conservatives rallied and demanded restoration of religious law and the sultan's authority. In response, the Young Turks organized the Turkish army in Macedonia and marched on Istanbul, where they deposed Sultan Abdülhamid in April 1909. They placed the sultan's ineffective brother on the throne as Sultan Mehmed V and took complete control of the government.

Mustafa Kemal played an important role in these events: he served as chief of staff of the army that marched on Istanbul. Although the Young Turks' swift military success was due in large part to Kemal's abilities, Enver was the public hero once again. Disappointed at remaining in the shadows while his rival enjoyed the spotlight, Kemal turned his back on politics and devoted himself entirely to military affairs. Recognition was yet to come.

4

War and Defeat

The lessons Mustafa Kemal learned from his time with the Young Turks were harsh. One was that good ideas alone do not assure political success. Another was that the best men — at least those Kemal considered best — do not always become leaders. Kemal believed that men like Enver, who were being widely acclaimed as the leaders of the new Turkey, were unworthy of their popularity. He was convinced that he himself should take their place.

For now Kemal focused on toughening the Turkish forces. War with the non-Turkish residents of the empire — or with Europe — was possible at any time. He was convinced that the fate of the Ottoman Turkish state depended on the strength of its army. When a senior general asked for his help in putting down a revolution in Albania, Kemal developed the battle plan and crushed the revolt.

In 1911 the fortunes of the Ottoman Empire plunged. European competition for possession of territories on the Mediterranean coast of North Africa had become so heated in recent years that finally only Libya remained under Ottoman control.

For salvation and independence, there is no resolution or solution other than first combatting the enemy with all our might and defeating him.
—MUSTAFA KEMAL

During his youth, Mustafa Kemal dreamed of leading the decaying Ottoman Empire into a new future. As the empire faced one disaster after another in the early 20th century, the moment of his eventual triumph drew closer.

UPI/BETTMANN NEWSPHOTOS

Proud Turkish soldiers parade on horseback through city streets. Embittered by Enver's popularity, Kemal concentrated on strengthening the Ottoman army as the tumultous second decade of the 20th century began.

Then Italy decided to join the race for colonies, declared war on the Ottoman Empire, and invaded Libya. Although the Turks sent some of their best officers, including Enver and Kemal, the Ottoman government lost all of Libya, the island of Rhodes, and the Dodecanese Islands. These regions were quite close to the coast of Asia Minor, the heartland of the Ottoman Empire.

This dismal turn of events was quickly followed by an even worse disaster for the empire. The next year the small countries of the Balkan Peninsula formed an alliance and went to war with the goal of expelling the Turks from European soil permanently. They nearly succeeded. Lost forever to the Ottoman Empire in this short war were the cities of Monastir and Salonika, among others, and Mustafa Kemal's mother and sister were forced to flee to Istanbul with thousands of other Muslim Turkish refugees. Kemal was deeply shocked by these developments. Not only was his family uprooted and his birthplace lost, but the enemy was virtually at the gates of Istanbul itself.

Then came another catastrophe, from Kemal's perspective. The Turkish people were especially distraught over the Bulgarians' capture of Edirne in the Balkan War of 1912. The city had been the Ottoman capital during the 14th century and was the site of one of the grandest mosques in all the empire. The Turks were so enraged by the loss of the city that they violently overthrew the already tottering Turkish government. As if that were not disaster enough, the head of the three-man dictatorship that emerged as the new government in Istanbul was Kemal's old foe. When war broke out in the Balkans once again, Enver led the cavalry detachment that recaptured Edirne. Enver was considered a military hero and was now called "Pasha," a title of distinction.

Fewer than five years after the Young Turk Revolution of 1908 — which had ended Sultan Abdülhamid's repressive government — the Ottoman Empire was once again in the hands of a dictatorship. The new regime was suspicious of Kemal. Once again he was exiled, this time to Sofia, Bulgaria, where he was to be military attaché to the Ottoman embassy. Kemal enjoyed an active social life in Sofia, which offered the enticements of European culture, such as an opera house, theaters, and nightclubs.

The harbor of Rhodes, an island that was lost, along with Ottoman territory in North Africa, after a 1911 war with Italy. Once a dominant force in the region, the empire was quickly becoming a casualty of European expansionism.

This latest period of exile was not wasted on frivolities, however. Slowly and methodically, Kemal began to lay the foundations for a program of reform for his own country. He traveled through Bulgaria observing the Turkish minority. Whenever he could he tried to instill in these people a sense of their identity as Turks. He also carefully studied the Bulgarian parliament.

Not all of Kemal's experiences in Bulgaria were so positive — he also fell victim to the common European prejudice against Turks. The young officer fell in love with Dimitrina Kovatcheva, daughter of the Bulgarian minister of war. He courted her at parties and dances and hoped to impress her with talk of his plans for the westernization of Turkey and the emancipation of Turkish women from restrictive Muslim traditions. Dimitrina returned his affections, but his hopes of marrying a sophisticated European woman were ruined when her father rejected him as a suitor. For the prominent Bulgarian Christian, the marriage of his daughter to a Muslim Turk was simply unthinkable.

Victorious Greek troops march through a conquered city during the Balkan Wars. In October 1912 Greece, Montenegro, Bulgaria, and Serbia joined forces against the Ottoman Empire, scoring many quick victories and depriving the empire of much of its territory in Europe.

Other dark clouds were appearing as well. Although Enver Pasha was proving to be an effective reformer back in Istanbul, his energetic efforts were to be cut short. War loomed on the horizons of Europe, and the Ottoman Empire was soon to be fatally caught up in the gathering storm.

On June 28, 1914, a successful terrorist plot in a remote Balkan town sparked flames of war that quickly engulfed much of the world. The great catastrophe began when Archduke Franz Ferdinand, crown prince of the Austro-Hungarian Empire, was assassinated on an official visit to Sarajevo, the capital city of the Austro-Hungarian province of Bosnia. The assassin was a member of a Serbian terrorist group popularly known as the Black Hand.

The Serbian nationalists opposed Austria's attempts to gain influence in the Balkan countries once ruled by the Ottoman Turks. They were afraid that Austria would make Serbia a colony. The Ser-

Edirne became the focus of Turkish patriotism following the city's capture by the Bulgarians in 1912. When Enver, Kemal's rival, liberated the city the following year, his popularity soared.

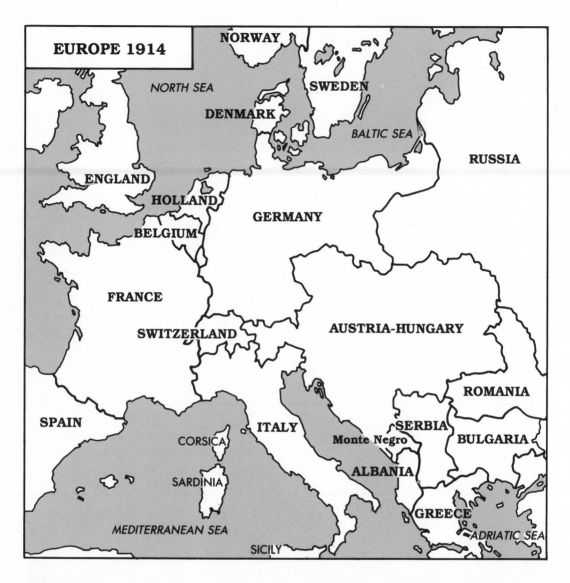

EUROPE 1914

NORWAY
NORTH SEA
SWEDEN
DENMARK
BALTIC SEA
RUSSIA
ENGLAND
HOLLAND
BELGIUM
GERMANY
FRANCE
AUSTRIA-HUNGARY
SWITZERLAND
ROMANIA
SPAIN
ITALY
SERBIA
BULGARIA
CORSICA
Monte Negro
SARDINIA
ALBANIA
MEDITERRANEAN SEA
GREECE
SICILY
ADRIATIC SEA

Map of Europe in 1914, the year that World War I began. The defeat of Austria-Hungary and its allies — Germany, Turkey, and Bulgaria — would significantly alter the map of Europe.

bians were supported by the Russians, who had plans of their own to control the entire Balkan Peninsula and thus gain strategic access to the Mediterranean. Russian ambitions in the Balkans were therefore a threat to the Ottoman Turks on the one hand, and to Austria and other central European countries on the other.

Austria blamed the Serbians for the murder of the heir to the throne, and many countries were outraged at the terrorist attack. Finally, after a month of demands and threats by the Austrians against the Serbians, the Austro-Hungarian Empire declared war on Serbia. Alarmed, Russia threatened to move against Austria, whereupon Germany, an ally of Austria, declared war against Russia. Six weeks after the assassination, France, England, and even Japan were drawn into the war against Germany and Austria. World War I had begun.

The situation was extremely dangerous for the Ottoman Empire. The main question was whether the Turks should remain neutral or enter the war on the side of the Central Powers (Germany, Austria-Hungary, and Bulgaria) to help fight Russian domination of the Balkan Peninsula. Some, including Enver, thought the war would be short and that the Ottoman Turks should join in quickly in order to profit from a victory by the Central Powers.

Others, such as Mustafa Kemal, argued for Turkish neutrality. They felt they could not count on a German victory and thought the war would be long and costly. Even if the Central Powers were victorious, they feared that Germany might seize Turkish territory, reducing the once great empire to a mere satellite country. And if the Central Powers lost, the Turks would be punished by Russia and her allies. The Ottoman Empire might well cease to exist, and Turks would fall under foreign domination, most likely by Russia in particular.

Enver, as minister of war, was in an excellent position to push the Ottoman government toward war. In the first few days of the war two German navy cruisers arrived in Istanbul. Instead of disarming them according to the rules of the empire's official neutrality, Enver arranged a ruse. He arranged to "buy" the battleships from the German government and added them to the Ottoman navy, although the German crews remained on the ships. Then the cruisers proceeded to the Black Sea for maneuvers. Enver and his German friends hoped that the Russians would attack so that he could persuade his government to join the war. When the Russians held back, an imperial Turkish fleet, including the two German cruisers, finally attacked a series of Russian ports without warning—and with-

The 1914 assassination of Archduke Franz Ferdinand, the heir to the throne of the Austro-Hungarian Empire, began the chain of events that quickly escalated into World War I. After the outbreak of war, Enver was eager to join Austria and the Central Powers.

ART RESOURCE

Russian and Ottoman troops do battle in 1915. Although the Turkish forces fought tenaciously on the Russian front, they were losing when the Russian Revolution of 1917 caused Russia to withdraw from World War I.

out the knowledge of most of the ministers of the Ottoman government. The Ottoman Empire had entered World War I.

Although Mustafa Kemal, now a lieutenant colonel, had favored Turkish neutrality, his fierce patriotism led him to support the war effort strongly once it had begun. Though Kemal was eager to command troops in combat, Enver insisted that he remain in Sofia.

Meanwhile, Enver himself traveled east to lead the Ottomans against Russia in the mountainous Caucasus border region. He dreamed of defeating the Russians and bringing the Muslims of central Asia under Ottoman rule. He also wanted to invade Persia and to threaten British rule in India by urging Indian Muslims to rebel against the British.

These were utterly fantastic ideas, however. The Ottoman army had not recovered from the Balkan Wars and was ill matched against such major powers as Russia and Great Britain. The bulk of Enver's army in the Caucasus was wiped out during a single bitter winter.

Humbled by this disastrous defeat, Enver finally agreed to allow Kemal to assume command of a new division of troops about to be organized in the Gallipoli region, just west of Istanbul. As Kemal had pointed out, it was quite possible that the British might try to land troops there in an effort to crush the Ottoman Empire and open routes between the western powers and their Russian allies.

Enver's appointment of Kemal to Gallipoli turned out to be crucial for both the Ottoman Empire and Mustafa Kemal himself. The British did attack Gallipoli, and the ensuing battle established Kemal's reputation as a courageous soldier and clever strategist. Instead of pursuing impossible dreams as Enver had done, Kemal stuck to realistic assessments of what the Turkish army could accomplish and refused to go beyond them. According to a British historian, "Seldom in history . . . can the exertions of a single divisional commander have exercised . . . so profound an influence not only on the course of a battle, but perhaps on the fate of a campaign and even the destiny of a nation." Kemal's prestige also was enhanced because his accomplishment was so unusual, for the Battle of Gallipoli was one of the very few occasions when an Ottoman army defeated European forces during World War I.

Mustafa Kemal was promoted to colonel, then general (which entitled him to be addressed as "Pasha"), and sent to the Russian front. The war went badly for his troops, who suffered terribly from lack of food and other supplies. As defeat seemed imminent, the Ottoman armies were saved by a momentous event beyond their control. In March 1917 the Russian tsar was overthrown in a revolution that eventually transformed Russia into the Soviet Union. The Russians dropped out of the war.

Kemal was put in command of the Seventh Army, which was to be the nucleus of a major force commanded by Germans and given the dramatic name of "Thunderbolt." The official goal was the recapture of the city of Baghdad from the British, but Kemal knew the situation was hopeless. The Ottoman forces were inadequate to achieve this goal, Kemal argued, and should be saved to defend the empire's heartland, Asia Minor.

> *If you consider me unworthy to become an officer of the first rank, please tell me so openly.*
> —MUSTAFA KEMAL
> to Enver, after Enver denied his request to serve at the front

Kemal further argued against keeping German officers in command of the Turkish army. "The Germans should not be allowed to prolong this war to the point of reducing Turkey to the position of a colony in disguise," he wrote in a long, bold report that also severely criticized the government in Istanbul for being corrupt and having lost the support of the war-weary people. He predicted that the royal house of Osman itself might "collapse suddenly from within." Kemal resigned his command of the Seventh Army and returned to Istanbul. Only his popularity as a war hero saved him from government retribution.

As the British advanced into Syria in 1917, Arab nationalist troops rose up in rebellion against Turkish rule. In desperation, Sultan Mehmed V reassigned Kemal to the command of the army in Syria. But the Allies were unstoppable, and by late October 1918, the last major battle between the Allies and the Ottoman Empire was fought north of Aleppo, Syria. On October 30, an armistice was signed, and World War I ended for the Ottoman Turks. The Allies — Russia, France, Great Britain, Japan, Italy, Greece, and the United States—had triumphed.

The once great empire was reduced to a territory about the size of the state of Texas, limited almost exclusively to the peninsula of Asia Minor plus the city of Istanbul on the European shore of the Bosporus River. Nor were the Turks given any assur-

Conquering British troops entered Baghdad, Syria, on March 11, 1917. Before this date, Baghdad had been one of the most important cities in the Ottoman Empire.

THE BETTMANN ARCHIVE

ance that even this shrunken "empire" would remain in Turkish hands. The British, French, Italians, and Greeks all had ambitions to colonize parts of Asia Minor. It seemed only a matter of time until all would be lost.

A thick mantle of doom enveloped Istanbul. No one knew what to expect; everyone prepared for the worst. The coming winter promised to be cold, dark, and difficult. Coal, which was needed to heat homes and run steamships, had virtually disappeared. Public transportation was almost at a standstill. Main streets were badly lit; side streets were not lit at all. Criminals thrived, and ordinary people ventured out at night only with pistols at their sides. Policemen were hard to find and frequently corrupt. Prices, especially for food, were soaring. In desperation, some Turks denied their nationality. They avoided wearing the traditional Turkish brimless hat, the *fez*, and tried to find work with the victorious Allied forces that were moving into the city.

The world seemed to have been turned upside down. Christian subjects of the Ottoman sultan were given positions of official responsibility by the Allied occupiers, and Muslim Turks, the proud builders and governors of a great 600-year-old empire, were reduced to lowly status. Three of the most prominent leaders of the Young Turk movement fled the country, leaving the job of governing under enemy control to others.

The Allies prepared to divide up the Ottoman Empire. In a series of secret treaties, they had agreed that the Russians would take over the city of Istanbul and the area around the Straits of the Dardanelles and the Bosporus, thus securing their control of the Black Sea once and for all. The British would seize Iraq and Palestine; the French, Syria; and the Italians, a portion of the southwestern coastal area of Asia Minor. Some of these provisions were changed, however. The new revolutionary government of Russia declared that it totally rejected the colonialist ambitions of the tsar, so the British led the Allied occupation of Istanbul and proposed to put the city and the surrounding area under international administration.

> *I have ambitions, and even very great ones; however, they do not consist in material satisfactions. . . . I seek the realization of these ambitions in the success of a great idea which, while profiting my country, will give me the keen satisfaction of a duty worthily accomplished.*
> —MUSTAFA KEMAL

45

THE BETTMANN ARCHIVE

Two Turkish men outside a mosque in Anatolia. After the Allies occupied Ottoman territories, Christians fared better than Muslims.

In addition, the Greeks, who had joined the war on the side of the Allies in 1917, demanded what they thought was their just reward. They wanted control over large territories on the Black Sea and in western Asia Minor, centered on the city of Smyrna. This region had been the site of great ancient Greek city-states, such as Ephesus, Troy, and Sardis, and was still inhabited by hundreds of thousands of ethnic Greeks.

The Armenians, who had long been at odds with the Ottoman government and had suffered severely, especially during World War I, claimed large portions of eastern Asia Minor, where they hoped to establish an independent state. Greeks and Armenians, especially, based their claims on the principle of national self-determination, which President Woodrow Wilson of the United States had proclaimed as the only fair basis for settling disputes over territory after World War I.

All these ambitions were written into a treaty that the Allies forced the government of the sultan to sign at Sèvres, a French town near Paris. In effect the Ottoman Empire would be reduced to a small landlocked area in central Asia Minor. It would become a dependent colony in all but its ironic name.

Some Turks, Mustafa Kemal included, had other ideas. Though the armistice required the disbanding of armies and the surrender of weapons, many officers hid their weapons or turned them over to national resistance groups, which began to form as the Allied occupation troops moved in.

On May 15, 1919, yet another disaster befell the Turks. A Greek army landed at the Aegean seaport of Smyrna under the eyes of the British, French, and American navies. The Greek prime minister meant to use this opportunity to reestablish Greek rule in Asia Minor; he ultimately hoped to bring even the imperial capital of Istanbul, which the Greeks called Constantinople, under Greek domination. Greek troops moved inland, capturing far more territory than the Allies had agreed to, and unleashing violence against the Turkish population wherever they went. Protests from the Istanbul government were ignored.

Nothing could have been better calculated to inflame the Turks of Asia Minor. The territorial losses before this could all be accepted because they involved lands primarily inhabited by non-Turks — either Christian nationalities, as in the Balkans; or Muslim Arabs, as in Mesopotamia, Syria, and Palestine. Even the foreign occupation of the capital, Istanbul, could be accepted, for the soldiers of the victorious Allies would sooner or later withdraw. But Asia Minor was Turkish soil, and the Greeks, unlike the British and French, were not powerful Europeans. Rather, they were a people who had been conquered by the Ottoman Empire in 1456 and had lived as subjects of the empire for centuries. Greek conquest of western Asia Minor would be an intolerable national humiliation.

Masses of Turks protested in the streets, even under the very eyes of the European occupiers of Istanbul. The sultan himself wept when he received the news. Everywhere the call went out: someone should do something — anything — to stop this insufferable outrage. The situation was ripe for the emergence of an energetic leader. The day after the Greek landing, Mustafa Kemal boarded the Turkish ship *Bandirma* and sailed into the Black Sea bound for the northern port of Samsun, where he had been assigned to restore order following outbreaks of violence between Greeks and Turks.

THE BETTMANN ARCHIVE

American president Woodrow Wilson was one of the architects of the peace terms that concluded World War I. Although he had called for a "peace without victory" in order to lessen the dissatisfaction of the vanquished, the Ottoman Empire did not see the fruits of this policy.

5

Challenges and Triumph

Mustafa Kemal landed at Samsun on May 19, 1919. Although his official mission was to restore order, his true goal was to capitalize on the Turkish resentment of the Greeks and lead a rebellion against the European-controlled government. When the newly appointed 38-year-old inspector general stepped onto the flimsy wooden pier at 7:00 on that fateful misty morning, hardly anyone seemed to notice. Yet this was the moment for which he had long prepared. Now was his chance to begin to carry out the ideas for social and political reform that he had debated and discussed for more than 20 years. May 19 thus was a major turning point both in Kemal's life and in Turkish history. He later made it his official birthday, and the day is still celebrated as a national holiday.

When Kemal arrived, the situation was desperate, but in his opinion, not hopeless. For one thing, he was extremely confident of his ability to accomplish great feats. For another, he had in his pocket a set of orders from the Allied-controlled Istanbul government that gave him broad authority over both mil-

> *With this armistice, the Ottoman Empire was not only consenting to capitulate unconditionally before its enemies, but promised, as well, to assist them to occupy the country.*
> —MUSTAFA KEMAL
> on the Armistice of 1918

Although the sultan and the Allied occupiers of the empire sent him to Samsun to restore order, Kemal did just the opposite: after his arrival on May 19, 1919, he began to fuel the flames of Turkish resentment that would eventually propel him to power.

THE BETTMANN ARCHIVE

Ottoman sultan Mehmed VI had Kemal declared a religious outlaw when he set up a rival government. It was officially decreed that whoever killed Kemal would be assured a place in heaven.

itary and government officials. Furthermore, the interior of Asia Minor was remote from the centers of Allied power; the few officers the Allies had posted in provincial towns would need many reinforcements in order to overcome active resistance. Though the Turkish troops were exhausted and disorganized, several units remained intact, and at least two were commanded by Kemal's friends.

Aware that he needed massive popular support to carry out his revolt, he was careful to hide his own antireligious and antigovernment feelings so that he could appeal to the piousness and loyalty of the ordinary Turk. One of his first acts as inspector general was to urge local officials and religious leaders throughout the country to organize large public meetings to protest foreign encroachment on the empire's territory, especially by the Greeks.

The government in Istanbul and the British occupiers, fearing that Kemal was about to organize a rival government, dismissed him from his position as inspector general and forbade the officials in Asia Minor to obey his orders. Kemal resigned from the army, so that in the future he would not be directly disobeying the government. If he could avoid arrest and imprisonment, he would be able to carry on his political activities as a civilian. His resignation was painful, for the army had been his life ever since he entered military school in Salonika. Kemal also wondered if he could command respect without the uniform that symbolized the authority of the Ottoman sultan.

The key to Kemal's success was Kiazim Karabekir, an associate of Kemal's from the days of the Young Turk Revolution. He had been ordered to arrest Kemal and take over his job as inspector general. Kemal was tremendously relieved when Kiazim greeted him with a smart salute and said, "You are still our honored commander, as you were in the past. I have brought your official carriage and cavalry escort. We are, all of us, at your orders, Pasha."

Bolstered by Kiazim's support, Kemal called together a congress of representatives from the entire country who met in Sivas. The delegates decided to form the Association for the Defense of the Rights of Anatolia (Asia Minor) and Rumelia (the European part of the Ottoman Empire). Mustafa Kemal was elected chairman of the executive committee. The congress backed his program, which called for the preservation of the Ottoman state headed by the sultan. Kemal's program also reaffirmed the equal legal rights of Muslims and non-Muslims in that state and declared that because the government in Istanbul was controlled by foreign powers, the newly forming nationalist movement would rescue the sultan and protect the provinces of eastern Anatolia from foreign intervention.

When the government held elections for a new parliament in 1919, Kemal was elected. Fearing arrest, he did not take his seat, because parliament met in Allied-controlled Istanbul. Instead he moved his headquarters to Angora, a town conveniently situated so that Kemal was able to meet with many of the newly elected representatives as they made their way to the capital.

The Istanbul parliament adopted Kemal's nationalist program in full on February 17, 1920, giving it the official name of the National Pact. For the first time, the lawmaking body of the Ottoman Turkish government declared its willingness to give up ter-

Motorcars and oxen share the streets of Angora, the city Kemal selected for his opposition government. By the end of his lifetime, he would transform the city into a modern metropolis.

ritories in which Turks were a minority, such as Mesopotamia, Syria, and Palestine. Mustafa Kemal and his supporters were making clear to the world that they wished to transform the Ottoman Turkish state into a national unit rather than a multinational empire. In return, they asked that the world allow them to retain their independence without interference.

The Allies, however, would not agree. They forced Sultan Mehmed VI (who succeeded to the sultanate after his brother Mehmed V's death in 1918) to dis-

Greek soldiers take aim at the enemy during their war with the Turks in 1921. Although Kemal's nationalist government had recently scored many military and diplomatic successes, he knew that the conflict between the two nations would not be easily resolved.

AP/WIDE WORLD PHOTOS

solve the parliament, arrest its nationalist members, declare martial law in Istanbul, and allow Allied troops to replace the Turkish police. The sultan went even further. He had the chief religious authority in the land declare Kemal and his supporters infidels and condemn them to death. According to the Muslim religion, following this judgment was a religious duty; whoever carried out the death sentence was guaranteed a place in paradise. Needless to say, Kemal had to be on guard constantly.

Mustafa Kemal greets Halide Edib, known as the "Joan of Arc" of Turkey for her participation in the Turkish nationalist movement. Edib rode alongside Kemal's triumphant army as it entered Smyrna on the heels of the fleeing Greeks.

The sultan's wish to be rid of Mustafa Kemal and his supporters was difficult to fulfill, however. About 100 nationalist members of the parliament, including its elected president, managed to escape the Allied dragnet. They made their way to Angora, where, along with 190 newly elected nationalist representatives, they reconvened as the Grand National Assembly on April 23, 1920. They declared that the dissolution of the Istanbul parliament was illegal and claimed that "the real authority in the country is the national will as represented by the assembly." The Grand National Assembly elected Mustafa Kemal president and established a committee to draft a new constitution.

The members of the assembly also declared that they hoped to free the sultan from foreign control and restore him to his rightful place — within a constitutional system that would restrict his authority. But there was no longer any doubt that revolution was in the air and that the sultan's days were numbered. As Kemal had hoped, the Turkish people were moving gradually but steadily away from their traditional loyalties.

Although the nationalist movement was full of promise in the spring of 1920, it faced a very uncertain future. Problems were everywhere. Despite the movement's broad support — from army officers, political leaders, writers, journalists, and ordinary Turkish citizens — the movement was strongly opposed by the sultan and his government in Istanbul. In the east, Armenian forces were determined to establish an Armenian state in Asia Minor. In the south, the French were stirring up the Christian population against the Turks, giving rise to bitter fighting and some massacres. In the west, a large Greek army was poised to advance even farther into the interior in hopes of establishing a new Greek empire.

Realizing that he did not have enough armed and trained soldiers to deal with all of these problems at once, Kemal tried to concentrate on Turkey's dispute with the Armenian nationalists first. With arms from the revolutionary communist government of Russia, he pushed the Armenian forces out of Asia Minor. The Armenians signed an armistice with the Turkish nationalists. (Shortly afterward, the Russian communists succeeded in subverting the government, and Armenia became part of the Soviet Union.)

Other successes followed. At about the same time, the French, exhausted by the guerrilla warfare that plagued their part of Asia Minor, asked Kemal for an armistice. He was happy to agree, because this peace agreement would end pressure on another front and gain his government recognition by one of the European great powers. Next, the Italians, who also had been active in Asia Minor of late, decided to abandon their own activities there. Finally the army sent by the Istanbul government to fight Kemal's nationalist forces disintegrated without winning any important battles.

By the beginning of 1921 most of Kemal's enemies had been pushed back, defeated, or neutralized — with one exception. The Greek army, the nationalists' most dangerous enemy, had yet to be confronted. The Greeks had made big gains against the Turks, and by July 1921, they were threatening the

> *The nation remained indifferent to its destiny, while its enemies . . . were about to dismember the country. Fortunately, however, certain events caused our beloved nation to awaken and to regain its vigilance.*
> —MUSTAFA KEMAL
> on the Turkish reaction to the Greek invasion

THE BETTMANN ARCHIVE

The streets of Smyrna bustle
with commercial activity in
1925, three years after much
of the city was destroyed in
the wake of the Greek retreat
from Ottoman territory.

nationalist capital at Angora. In a near panic, the
Grand National Assembly made preparations to
evacuate the city. Some blamed Mustafa Kemal for
the desperate situation in which the Turks now
stood; they wanted to reduce his powers and force
him to take the advice of others, which the proud
nationalist leader often ignored. Kemal offered the
assembly a deal: if the Grand National Assembly
would grant him supreme command of both the
army and the government and allow him to rule
single-handedly in its name for three months, he
would assume full responsibility for whatever might
happen. The assembly agreed to Kemal's offer and
made him supreme commander.

Kemal vowed that "not an inch of the country
should be abandoned until it was drenched with
the blood of its citizens." He immediately ordered
all private citizens to donate supplies to the army.
Women were permitted to volunteer for military service, something unheard of among Muslims. They
performed heroically, carrying military supplies to
the front on their backs because motor trucks and

ox-carts were in short supply.

The Battle of the Sakarya began on August 23, 1921, and raged for three weeks. The crucial action took place at the town of Haymana, only 25 miles south of Angora, where Greeks and Turks fought continuously for eleven days. Finally on September 13 the Greek army was in full retreat, and Angora was saved. Mustafa Kemal returned to the nationalist capital in triumph and was rewarded by the Grand National Assembly. The assembly bestowed Mustafa Kemal Pasha with the additional title of *Gazi*, which means "fighter against the infidel."

The victory at Sakarya did not end the war against the Greeks, but it served as notice that Kemal's nationalist government in Angora was there to stay. The French and the Italians now officially recognized the Turks' insistence that the territory of Asia Minor not be divided without regard to the wishes of its inhabitants. The two countries signed formal agreements with Kemal's government giving up all claims to territory in Asia Minor.

It was now only a matter of time before the final

battle in the Greek-Turkish war would be fought, a battle that would decide at last the fate of the Turks in Asia Minor. Kemal wanted to take his time before his next attack on the Greek army. His troops were still physically weak and had few supplies, so he took a year to prepare for a final offensive. During that time he rejected offers of a new and more favorable peace treaty from the Allies and fended off attempts within the Grand National Assembly to restrict his powers.

Finally all was in readiness. The attack that Kemal hoped would end Greek occupation of Asia Minor forever was to begin the next day. He had selected the time and the place carefully. Crops that could provide food for the Greek troops and horses were still unharvested. The rainy season had not yet begun; thus the dry stream beds would be easily crossed by the attacking Turks. The movement of the Turkish troops had been carefully camouflaged so that the Greeks would be caught by surprise. As the Turks, who had fought nothing but defensive wars for over a decade, were about to begin this crucial offensive, Kemal issued an inspiring order: "Soldiers, your goal is the Mediterranean!"

At dawn on August 26, 1922, the attack began near the small town of Dumlupinar. Most of the Greek soldiers were still asleep in their tents when the Turkish forces charged. Within a few hours key Greek positions were captured, and thousands of Greek troops were threatened with encirclement by the Turks. Mustafa Kemal personally observed the main actions from observation posts on the front lines; as at Gallipoli, he set an example for the rest of the Turkish officers.

A great victory was in the making. Four days after the offensive began, half of the Greek army had either been captured or killed. Equipment was completely lost or left behind, and what remained of the Greek army was in headlong retreat toward the Aegean seacoast.

Without leaders and without hope, the retreating Greek troops burned, looted, raped, and butchered their way through the towns in their path. "They went to pieces altogether," was the report of the British consul in Smyrna, leaving "a sickening record of bestiality and barbarity."

The Turkish conquest was complete, the Greek defeat devastating and humiliating. But even in victory, tragedy occurred. Amid the sporadic fighting a fire broke out on September 9 and, fanned by a strong wind, quickly flamed out of control. It raged for three days, demolishing half of the city before finally burning itself out.

For the Turkish nation, however, September 9, 1922, was still a glorious day to be remembered. Halide Edib, one of modern Turkey's first female political activists and writers, described the Turkish army's procession into Smyrna, headed by Mustafa Kemal: "Nine days had the men been in the saddle — fighting in the midst of and behind the Greek army. There had been no moment free from danger, from action; there had been no moment of rest. . . . The goal of the Turkish soldier . . . had nothing to do with particular lands and sea. It was an assertion of a people's will to live."

> *All humanity and the civilized world will finally recognize the legitimate rights of the Turkish nation which has no purpose other than to live independently, as any other civilized nation, within its national boundaries and free of foreign intervention.*
> —MUSTAFA KEMAL
> 1921

6

End of an Empire, Birth of a Republic

Mustafa Kemal Pasha had saved the Turkish nation and gained international recognition with a dramatic military victory. An armistice was signed with Greece on October 11, 1922, in the town of Mudanya. Kemal's government gained control over Istanbul, the Straits of the Dardanelles and the Bosporus, and eastern Thrace up to the Maritsa river. Kemal had rescued the Turkish heartland by giving up much of the territory claimed by the Ottoman Empire; now new challenges were waiting to be met.

As negotiations for a final peace treaty were about to begin in the Swiss city of Lausanne, Mustafa Kemal began turning his energies toward the internal reforms he had longed to make since his days as a schoolboy. He carefully began to speak of reform in general terms, avoiding specifics. He encouraged the education of women and their increased participation in Turkish society. He warned against rejecting modern ideals. "You will be lepers, pariahs, alone in your obstinacy, with your customs of another age," he told his fellow Turks. "Remain yourselves, but learn how to take from the West what is indispensable to an evolved people."

> *It is only now that our real work is beginning.*
> —MUSTAFA KEMAL
> 1922

In 1922 Mustafa Kemal was widely regarded as the savior of the fragile Ottoman Empire. During the next few years, Kemal would prove himself worthy of his people's trust as he grappled with threats from abroad and at home.

UPI/BETTMANN NEWSPHOTOS

The city of Angora, home of Kemal's nationalist government. After the Allies invited both the Angora government and the sultan's regime in Istanbul to the bargaining table in Lausanne, Switzerland, Kemal succeeded in passing a law that abolished the sultanate in 1922.

When the Allies invited both the sultan's government in Istanbul and the government in Angora to the Lausanne peace conference, Kemal knew he must act decisively to further his nation's political evolution. He presented a motion to the Grand National Assembly declaring that the old government based on the sovereignty of the sultan had ceased to exist. However, Kemal's government would preserve the sultan's religious role as the caliph, the prophet Mohammed's representative on earth. The Grand National Assembly would elect a worthy member of the house of Osman, the dynasty that had ruled the Ottoman Empire for more than 600 years, to the caliphate. Kemal hoped to keep the country united, to turn its face from the past to the future, and yet to satisfy the traditional loyalty of the people to the house of Osman and the Muslim religion.

Still, strong resistance to such a radical change surfaced in the assembly, and a heated debate ensued. Losing patience with the hesitancy of the members of the assembly to dissolve the sultan's government, Kemal declared, "It was by violence that the sons of Osman acquired the power to rule over the Turkish nation and to maintain this rule for more than six centuries. It is now the nation that revolts against these usurpers, puts them in their place and actually carries on their sovereignty." If the members of the assembly did not agree, Kemal concluded ominously, "It is possible that some heads will be cut off." Opponents of the proposal, mostly religious leaders, got the point, and on November 1, 1922, the assembly unanimously voted to abolish the sultanate.

Two weeks later, the last Ottoman sultan, Mehmed VI, secretly fled Istanbul on a British warship and spent the rest of his life in exile in Europe. This was the undignified end of the illustrious Ottoman dynasty, which had struck fear in the heart of Christian Europe for most of the preceding six centuries. The Grand National Assembly then elected the sultan's pronationalist cousin, Abdülmecid II, caliph, with the understanding that he would exercise only religious and symbolic functions to be spelled out by the assembly.

With victory achieved and peace negotiations underway, the pressure on the Turks to maintain a united front seemed to slacken. Opposition to Mustafa Kemal began to surface in a more serious way. Among his opponents were Muslim religious leaders and those who feared that he might take advantage of his tremendous popularity to make himself dictator.

The two groups came together in December 1922 to support a measure that would oust Kemal from the assembly. The proposed bill would allow only those who had been born within the new borders of Turkey or who had established a permanent residence within those borders for at least five years to be elected to the Grand National Assembly. Kemal's birthplace, Salonika, was now part of Greece — and as a soldier and a general during a time of turmoil,

> *The Grand National Assembly of Turkey does not belong to the caliph. . . . [It] belongs to . . . the nation itself.*
> —MUSTAFA KEMAL
> 1923

63

he had not lived in any one place for as long as five years. Mustafa Kemal had to use all his powers of persuasion to convince the members of the assembly to reject this proposal, which was finally defeated.

Foreign relations demanded Kemal's constant attention as well. He had to make sure that the Allies, particularly Great Britain, did not take at the negotiating table in Lausanne what the Turks had won on the bloody battlefields of Asia Minor. The main issues at Lausanne were the definition of the borders of the new Turkey, payment of the country's foreign debt, and control of the financial system. The Turkish delegation to the peace conference was led by Ismet Pasha, one of Mustafa Kemal's closest associates and a man in whom he had great confidence. The Allied representatives tried to wrap up the negotiations quickly, and many treated the Turks as an inferior breed of people to whom they could dictate whatever they wished. As a result, the peace conference broke down early in February 1923. Ultimately, however, the Allies were unwilling to go to war against the Turks again. Thus, after considerable bargaining over details, the Treaty of Lausanne was signed on July 24, 1923.

Holding the two symbols of his faith — the Koran and the sword — Mohammed, the prophet of Islam, stands before the holy city of Mecca. Kemal's popularity with Turkish Muslims would decline as he began instituting widespread secular reforms.

THE BETTMANN ARCHIVE

Ismet Pasha represented the empire during the long, difficult bargaining process that took place in Lausanne. The Turkish diplomat shared Kemal's resentment of the widespread prejudice against Turks, and defiantly stood up to the European representatives at the conference.

This treaty represented another big success for the Turks; they had forced the Allies to deal with them for the first time on a basis of mutual respect and dignity. The recognized borders of the new Turkey were virtually the same as they are today, encompassing the heartland in which the overwhelming majority of the population was Turkish. The only concession made by the Turks — and it proved to be a large one — was in giving up an area known as the Mosul, which became part of Iraq, then under British control. The area included extremely valuable oil fields that the British were determined to keep for themselves. To signify their acceptance of the new borders, the Turks agreed to renounce "all rights and title whatsoever over . . . the territories situated outside the frontiers laid down in the present treaty. . . ."

The Turks also made concessions on the important issue of control of the Straits of the Dardanelles and the Bosporus. They accepted the demilitarization of the area and the creation of an international commission that would control shipping through this critical waterway. On this issue the Lausanne Treaty turned out to be only temporary. Thirteen years later a new treaty was negotiated that returned the Straits region to full Turkish control, with a guarantee of freedom of passage for commercial (unarmed) ships of all nations.

TURKISH CULTURE AND INFORMATION OFFICE, N.Y.

Once in power, Kemal surprised some of his supporters by setting up a government that resembled a dictatorship more than a democracy. In 1923 he established the People's Republican party, a group that approved his political proposals simply as a matter of course.

The treaty also paved the way for a compulsory exchange of populations between Greece and Turkey. Ultimately almost 1.5 million Greek-speaking inhabitants of Asia Minor, excluding those living in the city of Istanbul, were obliged to move to Greece. In exchange nearly half a million Muslim inhabitants of Greece — most of them Turks — were sent to Turkey. Though the uprooting of 2 million people was brutal, the arrangement solidified the peace between Greece and Turkey by removing minorities whose treatment might have disturbed future relations between the two countries.

Finally, the Lausanne Treaty ended the special legal status non-Turkish and non-Muslim minorities had enjoyed, especially during the days of Allied occupation. This provision particularly pleased Mustafa Kemal, who had resented the special status that non-Turks had profited from under Allied rule.

The Lausanne Treaty was a remarkable diplomatic victory for Kemal and his government. As the historian Bernard Lewis wrote, "Turkey, alone among the defeated powers of the First World War, succeeded in rising from her own ruins and, rejecting the dictated peace imposed on her by the victors, secured the acceptance of her own terms." This accomplishment was in large part the personal achievement of Mustafa Kemal.

After World War I, Kemal's former rival Enver Pasha was killed in Central Asia in a futile attempt to rally the Muslim peoples there to the cause of Turkish nationalism. Mustafa Kemal would have nothing to do with such farfetched dreams. Although he was a brilliant military leader, he also had the uncommon gift of political realism.

During the Lausanne peace negotiations, two major changes occurred in Mustafa Kemal's private life. First, on January 14, 1923, Kemal's mother, Zübeyde, died. Their relationship had often been stormy, even in early childhood. As Kemal had matured and become a dashing military officer, his mother had repeatedly criticized his life-style — especially his drinking habits and the company he kept. She also fretted about his political activities, which often put him in danger of arrest, imprisonment, and exile. In spite of these many disagreements, however, Kemal remained unfailingly loyal and was greatly saddened by her passing.

The second major change in Kemal's personal life happened shortly after his mother's death. On January 29, 1923, Mustafa Kemal married a socially prominent young Turkish woman named Latife. The marriage was full of symbolic meaning for the Turkish nation. Over the years Kemal had enjoyed the company of many women, but he was most fascinated by those who were well educated and emancipated in the western manner — who were not secluded in private or veiled in public as were most Muslim women.

His new wife was just such a modern woman — but, unlike all the other emancipated women he had met, Latife was Turkish. This fact, as well as her youth and beauty, made her intensely attractive to

> *There is but one power and that is national sovereignty. There is but one authority and that is the heart, the conscience, and the very existence of the nation itself.*
> —MUSTAFA KEMAL
> 1923

67

Kemal and his wife, Latife, in 1923, the year they were married. The couple divorced two years later, when Latife felt she could no longer tolerate Kemal's hard-drinking lifestyle and obsession with affairs of state.

him. In addition, Kemal knew that he would be able to hold her up as an example of the modern, educated, Turkish woman of the future.

The lovely and accomplished Latife, in turn, was infatuated with the dashing, handsome, 41-year-old savior of the Turkish nation. The two seemed perfectly suited. Unfortunately, the marriage quickly turned sour. Kemal and Latife scarcely had time for a meaningful private life. The first few months of their marriage were spent traveling through the country so that Kemal could make contact with the common people and begin to familiarize them gradually with his ideas of reform.

Latife became even more unhappy when the couple moved into the presidential home in Angora. Although the town had grown rapidly since Kemal first established his headquarters there four years earlier, it was still very provincial, with few advantages or distractions. Latife hated the long, late-night dinner conversations that were a hallmark of Mustafa Kemal's typical day in Angora. Kemal liked to invite close friends and co-workers to these nightly dinners so that they could discuss worldly affairs. Drink flowed as freely as the conversation, and loud talk and unruly behavior were common. At first Kemal wanted Latife to join in these evenings, so that he could show off his intelligent, emancipated wife. But Latife, who was used to refined, dignified behavior, particularly at the dinner table, made her distaste for these affairs very plain. When she began criticizing her husband in front of his friends, the proud Turk was infuriated.

As if all this were not enough, their relationship was jolted by the dramatic suicide of a woman named Fikriye, who had lived with Kemal before he married Latife. Although he had not really loved Fikriye, Kemal was shocked and upset by her death. On August 5, 1925, the unhappy couple divorced.

Although his private life was difficult, Kemal's entire program of reform was moving along very well. Widespread popular support enabled him to consolidate his power, so that his government began to look more like an "enlightened" dictatorship than a true democracy. When Kemal observed that the Grand National Assembly had become too unruly for him to easily control, he arranged for it to dissolve itself and called for national elections to create a new assembly. In order to guarantee his control over the newly elected representatives, he had already established a new political party, known as the People's Republican party. The new assembly came into being during the summer of 1923, just in time to ratify the Lausanne Treaty.

On October 9, 1923, the Grand National Assembly, at Kemal's urging, declared Angora to be the new capital of the country. This dramatic move signified that the new Turkey was turning its back on

> *If henceforward the women do not share in the social life of the nation, we shall never attain our full development.*
> —MUSTAFA KEMAL

the centuries-old tradition of imperial rule from the city of Istanbul. Before Istanbul was conquered by the Turks it had been known as Constantinople, the capital of the Byzantine (or Greek) Empire. The city's ties with Greek history encouraged Kemal to move the capital of Turkey out of Istanbul. He was also motivated by what he had seen when he was military attaché in Sofia, Bulgaria, just before the

Turkish soldiers storm Constantinople in 1453, the year the Ottoman Empire captured the city from the Greeks. The city, which was renamed Istanbul, served as the Ottoman capital for over 400 years, until Angora became the new capital in order to break ties with the empire's imperial past.

outbreak of World War I. Kemal's experiences in the Bulgarian capital sparked a grand dream of building a modern city to rival those of Europe. Plenty of room to build such a city existed in Angora, but not in Istanbul. Perhaps most important, Angora had become the symbol of Mustafa Kemal's nationalist movement ever since he had established his headquarters there in 1919.

Eventually most of Mustafa Kemal's dreams for the new national capital became realities. Wide, tree-lined boulevards were created, and imposing government buildings rose on the dry plateau. Modern apartment buildings were built along quiet residential streets, and a large public park was laid out near cultural centers. In 1930 the name of the city was officially changed to Ankara. By the 1980s its population was more than 2.5 million — more than 100 times its size when the rebellious Kemal first arrived there 60 years earlier. Modern Ankara contains numerous foreign embassies, a modern airport, three major universities, and such cultural institutions as a symphony orchestra, opera, ballet, and a number of theater companies.

Trolley cars and automobiles pass through the wide boulevards of Ankara, Turkey. This modern city, known as Angora until 1930, is a lasting testament to Kemal's commitment to national modernization.

From his youth onward, Western ideals of progress and democracy appealed to Kemal more than Muslim traditions.

Perhaps the most dramatic reform of all came toward the end of October 1923. The abolition of the sultanate and severe restrictions on the Muslim caliph who remained still did not achieve Kemal's purpose. His opponents continued to consider the caliph in Istanbul the true head of state, instead of merely a powerless figurehead. In order to clarify the situation decisively, Mustafa Kemal and a few close associates drafted yet another law, presented it to the Grand National Assembly, and were able to get it passed promptly. The law stated simply that "the form of government of the state of Turkey is a Republic . . . the President of Turkey is elected by the Grand National Assembly."

Fifteen minutes after this short but radical proposition passed, Mustafa Kemal was elected president of Turkey without a single vote of opposition. Truly, the Ottoman Empire was dead, and the Turkish Republic had been born. The date was October 29, 1923.

7

"The Six Arrows"

President Mustafa Kemal's Republic of Turkey was sickly at the time of its birth. Its population had suffered terribly during the wars of the past several years: some 2.5 million had died, leaving only about 13.2 million Turks within the borders of the new republic. The years of warfare and political upheaval had left despair throughout the land. Hundreds of thousands of Christian subjects of the old Ottoman Empire — especially Greeks and Armenians — had either fled the country or died. Only about 120,000 of nearly 2 million Greeks remained, and only about 100,000 of nearly 1.5 million Armenians. With so many members of Christian minorities gone, the economic life of which they had been a crucial part was almost at a standstill, and inflation brought sky-high prices everywhere. A great many villages, towns, and cities were in ruins, particularly in the west where the Greek soldiers destroyed as they retreated, and in the east where Turks, Russians, Armenians, and the agricultural people known as Kurds had waged terribly destructive battles. Kemal and his people faced an immense task, indeed.

> *I have always sided with one thing: I am for the Republic and for intellectual and social reforms.*
> —MUSTAFA KEMAL

Once the Ottoman Empire was officially dissolved and the Turkish republic born, Mustafa Kemal set about transforming national institutions. His basic program for reform, known as "The Six Arrows," would revolutionize Turkish society — sometimes against the will of the people themselves.

Mustafa Kemal wanted to create a government that would rely on a political philosophy distinct from the system of thought behind the communist Soviet Union to the north and from the free-market capitalist ideas in Europe and the United States. His program for Turkey thus became known as Kemalism; it consisted of six major ideas.

The first was the principle of *republicanism*. The new government was based not on personal rule by a single individual, such as the sultan, or of a hereditary ruling class, but on the principle of popular sovereignty. Each individual would have a say in the national government, and the will of the people would be expressed through the Grand National Assembly in Angora. The new slogan was "sovereignty belongs to the nation."

A Turkish official kisses President Kemal's hand in traditional greeting. Kemal worked to eradicate Eastern customs, but old traditions proved hard to break.

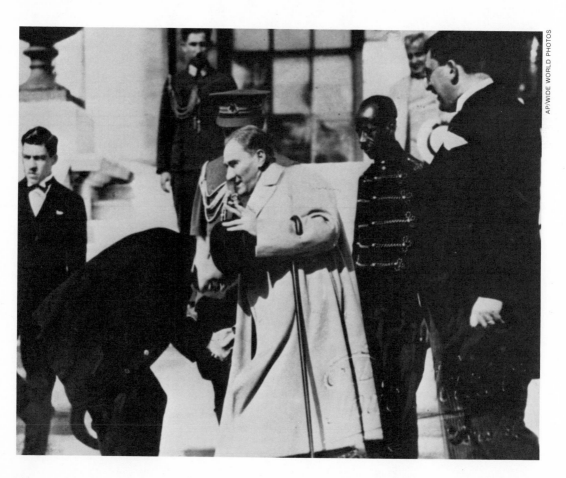

A Kurdish mother holds her child. One of President Kemal's principles for reform, *populism*, held that all the Republic's ethnic groups — including Kurds, Turks, and Christian minorities — were equal under the law.

The second principle of Kemalism was *nationalism*. The Ottoman Empire had been made up of many different peoples and was not officially associated with any of them. The empire's origins, language, and cultural heritage were certainly Turkish, but this identity had been virtually forgotten. Over the centuries, non-Turks or Turks who had distanced themselves from their ethnic origins had dominated the empire, until the name "Turk" had come to refer primarily to the poor, illiterate peasants in the rural villages — it was a term that had practically become an insult. Kemal set about convincing both educated city dwellers and illiterate villagers that they shared an identity as Turks, and that this identity was something of which they could be very proud. The terrible experience of the recent war with Greece and the brilliant victory that had finally been won by ordinary Turkish soldiers helped lay the groundwork for this newly developing national pride.

The third principle in the Kemalist program was *populism*. The Ottoman Empire had been based on a clear distinction between Muslims and non-Muslims (Christians and Jews); the new government adopted the modern western notion of the equality of all citizens, regardless of religion or ethnic background. The concept of one man—one vote was legally adopted. Turkey became the first Muslim nation in history to grant non-Muslims legal rights equal to those of Muslims.

The fourth principle was *revolutionism*. Mustafa Kemal was a leader in a hurry. He wanted to trans-

Peasants lead a caravan of camels down an isolated road in southern Turkey. One of Kemal's goals was to give rural peasants and urban workers a shared identity as Turks.

form the Turkish nation and society in a single generation. Gradual reform was out of the question: not only would it take too much time, it would provide opportunities for opponents to successfully resist change. As the program of the People's Republican party declared: "The party does not consider itself and the conduct of the state to be bound by principles of gradual and evolutionary development. The party deems it essential to remain faithful to, and to defend, the principles born of revolutions which our nation has made with great sacrifices."

THE BETTMANN ARCHIVE

Muslims worship in a Turkish mosque. Devout Muslims were upset by Kemal's insistence that state and religious functions be separated.

The fifth principle, *secularism*, was the most controversial of all the new government's goals, because the Turkish government had traditionally blended religion and politics. Kemal regarded Islam and its officials as ignorant of — and opposed to — the advances of modern science and technology. At the same time he was convinced that a nation could not survive in the 20th century without the benefits of

science. He therefore wanted to separate religion
from government as much as possible. In 1928 all
references to Islam as the official religion of Turkey
were removed from the constitution. Every citizen
could practice whatever religion he or she wished
in private and would enjoy complete legal equality.
Turkey was the first modern Muslim society to take
such a step.

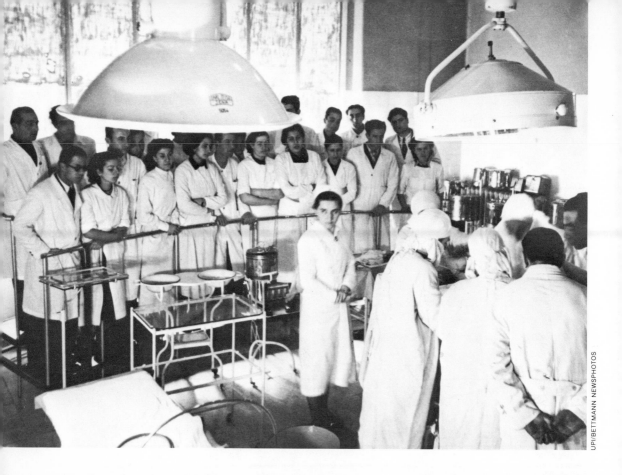

Doctors demonstrate modern surgical techniques in a new Turkish hospital. Improving medical technology was one of the ways Kemal hoped to bring his nation into the 20th century.

Finally, the sixth principle of Kemalism had to do with *government intervention in the economy*. Turkey was one of the first developing countries of Asia and Africa to wrestle with the problem of gaining not only political independence but also control of its own economy. Much of the economic life of the Ottoman Empire had been under the control of non-Muslims, and by the beginning of the 20th century, the European powers controlled much of the country's economy — including such crucial areas as the foreign debt, tariffs, and investments in major railroad, mining, and other enterprises. Kemal understood that Turkish political independence would mean little if control of the economy remained in the hands of foreigners who did not have to answer to the Turkish government. Since most minority and foreign businessmen had left the country during its recent years of unrest, Turkey now had to persuade them to come back and resume their economic activities under the new government, or find other sources of business know-how and investment in order to bring the Turkish economy back to life.

Mustafa Kemal strongly believed that Muslim Turks were just as capable of becoming successful businessmen as the empire's Christian minorities and foreigners from Europe had been. But most Turks had never been involved in high-level business activities, and they lacked experience and money. The minorities, for their part, were unwilling to return; foreigners were reluctant to risk their capital in a country ruled by a new and untried government. Mustafa Kemal was impatient; he was convinced that the economy had to be rebuilt as quickly as possible in order to overcome the poverty that plagued the country.

As a last resort Mustafa Kemal looked to the Turkish state to invest in economic activities that would restore national prosperity. Kemal claimed that he was not embracing communist principles; he was careful to point out that "statism," as he called this policy, left room for private enterprise, while communism did not allow individual economic activity.

Under statism, the Turkish government became the most important force in the Turkish economy. Government-owned investment banks were organized to finance enterprises such as mining and manufacturing. The effort would prove to be successful, but probably took longer than Mustafa Kemal expected — partly because of the worldwide depression of the 1930s. By the beginning of World War II in 1939, however, Turkey had developed mining enterprises in such minerals as iron, coal, copper, and chromium. With Soviet aid, a steel mill was built in the 1930s, and factories were built to manufacture such products as textiles, cement, and paper.

Kemal's six-point program was given the name of "The Six Arrows." The official symbol of the People's Republican party became a red banner emblazoned with six white arrows. Mustafa Kemal had done much to create the new Turk and the new Turkey; the Six Arrows, also his creation, outlined the way he wished both to be governed.

> *Every nation has its own traditions, mores, and national traits. No nation should imitate exactly another. Because if it does, it will really neither attain that identity nor preserve its own.*
> —MUSTAFA KEMAL

8

The Road of Reform

Announcing a program of reform is one thing; actually making changes happen is quite another. Many of his long time friends and associates objected to President Kemal's impatience with gradual change. They also were appalled to see that he was becoming an absolute dictator. Kemal felt he was confronted with a choice: he could heed his friends' advice to proceed slowly and follow democratic procedures, or he could ignore his valued colleagues, dispense with most democratic principles, and enact radical reforms on his own. Kemal wanted to take the second course, and he soon found an excuse to justify his actions.

In early 1925 an ethnic group called the Kurds, led by Sheikh Said, a religious tribal chief, declared open rebellion against the Turkish government. The sheikh denounced the anti-Muslim reforms of Kemal's government and urged his followers to launch a religious crusade to reestablish Islam in the national government. The Kurdish rebels managed to capture many rural villages and even a provincial

> *Reform signifies the tearing down of institutions which hampered the development of the Turkish nation for centuries.*
> —MUSTAFA KEMAL

A turbaned Muslim worshiper prepares to touch his head to the ground as part of the traditional prayer ritual. Kemal's attack on Islam included prohibiting Turks from wearing turbans in public. The brimmed hats he encouraged his countrymen to wear made it more difficult for Muslims to pray.

Curious onlookers view the body of a man who was hung for staging an unsuccessful attempt to assassinate President Kemal. Public execution was one of the means Kemal used to discourage opposition to his regime.

town. But Turkish military reinforcements quashed the revolt within several weeks. They rounded up the rebels, brought their leaders — including the sheikh — before special tribunals, and hanged them in the largest city of the region, Diyarbekir.

Although this revolt had not posed a serious threat to the young Turkish Republic, Kemal decided to use the atmosphere of crisis to eliminate his opposition completely. Members of the royal family of Osman had already been banished from

Turkey to ensure that they would not become the rallying point for antirevolutionary opposition. President Kemal used special emergency legal powers granted during the Kurdish revolt to attack his opponents. The crackdown centered on the Progressive Republican party, which had been organized by former friends who had become disillusioned with Kemal's leadership. He also made clear that at least for the time being, he did not believe democracy was the best system for Turkey.

Turkish schoolchildren of both sexes practice an armed drill. As part of Kemal's program to incorporate women into every aspect of modern Turkish society, military service became compulsory for women in 1936.

In 1925 Kurdish tribesmen, such as the man pictured here, staged a revolt against the Turkish republic. The uprising was quickly put down, but President Kemal used the unrest as an excuse to crack down on political opponents.

Given the conservatism of most of the people, he believed that he would not be able to carry out his ideas for modernization under a democracy. "It is necessary to take the nation by the hand," he announced. "Those who started the Revolution will complete it." Thus in the name of law, order, and national unity, he closed down many newspapers, banned the Progressive Republican party, and exiled—or hanged—leading critics.

Mustafa Kemal also delivered more deadly blows to traditional Islamic religion. He outlawed mystical religious orders, such as those that had been at the center of the Kurdish revolt. Religious schools were closed; henceforth, all education was to be under the tight control of the secular government through the Ministry of Education in Angora.

Kemal also attacked Islam in a more subtle way. The Islamic prayer ritual requires the faithful believer to kneel and touch his forehead to the ground while wearing a covering on his head. Kemal encouraged the assembly to pass a law that made it illegal to wear publicly the brimless turban or the tall red felt fez most Turkish men wore during their prayers. Instead, Kemal encouraged Turks to wear wide-brimmed Panama hats, in which it was certainly more difficult for Muslims to pray.

The political and social emancipation of women was also an important principle in Mustafa Kemal's reform program. He insisted that Turkish women deserved to be partners in his modern republic and asked his fellow Turks, "Is it possible that, while one half of a community stays chained to the ground, the other half can rise to the skies?" Kemal discouraged the practice of women wearing veils in public; according to Muslim tradition it was considered shameful for men outside a woman's family to see her face.

Kemal's far-reaching reforms eventually penetrated the Turkish language itself. The written Turkish language was very confusing and difficult to learn, which contributed to the nation's high illiteracy rate. President Kemal pushed for the adoption of the Latin alphabet used by western

If we did take advantage of the law concerning the reinforcement of peace and order, we did so . . . to show the visage of our nation as it really is and that it is not bigoted nor of a Middle-Ages mentality.
—MUSTAFA KEMAL
on the suppression of religion by his government

Kemal teaches a group of Turkish youths the fundamentals of the Latin alphabet. As part of his modernization program, a law calling for the adoption of this widely-used western alphabet was passed in 1928.

> *We cannot attempt to attain and surpass the level of contemporary civilization merely by boasting about our old civilization which reigned over the Old World.*
>
> —MUSTAFA KEMAL

Europeans, which he felt would simplify communication with fellow Turks and foreigners alike. In 1928 the use of the traditional alphabet was outlawed. Initially this drastic measure caused great confusion, but finally most Turks accepted it as an improvement.

Always seeking to boost national pride, Kemal next focused on Turkish history. He believed that a nation's morale is deeply affected by how it perceives its own past, and the history of the Ottoman Empire was hardly inspiring. Although its early centuries had been marked by pomp and glory, the later years,

90

Muslim women venture out in public wearing the veils prescribed by their religion. Kemal campaigned against this and other customs that restricted women, maintaining that if they did not "share in the social life of the nation, we shall never attain our full development."

especially the last century or so, were full of humiliation, corruption, and disgrace. Gone as completely as the glory days of the old empire were the millions of non-Turks in Europe and Asia who had once been ruled by the sultan. Kemal realized that in order to unite his countrymen behind the small nation that existed now, he had to present a noble vision of the Turkish past that emphasized the nation's heartland, Asia Minor.

Thus Mustafa Kemal directed the development of a new approach to Turkish history. Soon a textbook called *Outline of Turkish History* was published, modeled after the British writer H. G. Wells's famous book *Outline of History*, which Kemal greatly admired. The *Outline of Turkish History* emphasized

Students perform an experiment in a chemistry lab at Istanbul University. Whenever possible, Kemal's government encouraged the Turkish people — especially young people — to learn about science and technology.

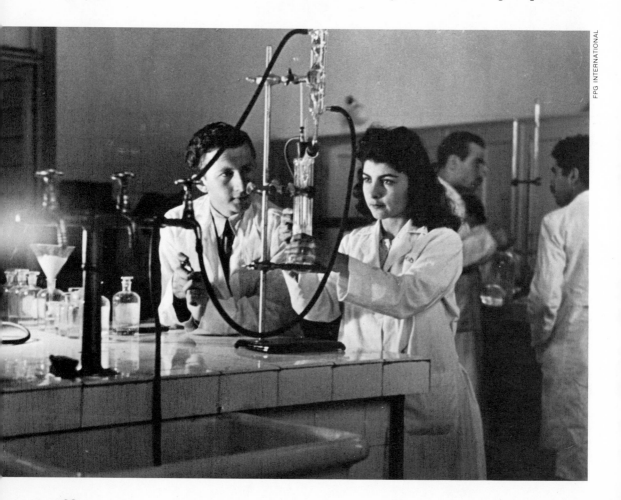

An avid student of western culture, Kemal admired the works of the British writer H. G. Wells. Kemal's program to heighten Turkish national pride included the publication of a history textbook modeled on Wells's highly-regarded *Outline of History*.

national accomplishments in politics, the arts, and other areas. It also put forth a controversial new doctrine meant to bolster national pride and counter the demoralizing effects of European prejudice — it claimed that all human civilization originated with the ancient Turks.

Historians today do not take this theory very seriously, but Mustafa Kemal would not mind in the least. His purpose was simply to instill pride and patriotism in the modern Turk—and he succeeded.

9

Father Turk

All was quiet in the Republic of Turkey that summer of 1930 when Mustafa Kemal first went public with his new idea. The last opposition party had been disbanded five years earlier, and the Kurdish revolt had been put down. Kemal's many reforms were in place, and the country seemed to have accepted them. President Kemal decided to introduce a more democratic system in place of his personal rule. He would create a legal opposition party to represent other points of view. He hoped this new experiment would silence Western criticisms of his one-party nation and revitalize the government by exposing it to the criticisms of an opposition party.

He summoned an old friend, Ali Fethi, who had been Turkish ambassador to France for the previous five years. Fethi was an admirer of parliamentary democracy and had closely observed the activities of the French parliament during his time in Paris. He was a political rival of longtime Prime Minister Ismet and was very critical of Ismet's rigid statist economic policies. Kemal persuaded Fethi to form an opposition party and assured him of his support. He also urged several of his trusted colleagues, including his own sister, Makbule, to join Fethi.

Atatürk was indeed the father of the Turks. The Turkey which now existed on a map, a compact whole salvaged from the wide-strewn fragments of the Ottoman Empire, was his creation.
—LORD KINROSS
British historian

President Mustafa Kemal valued reform over democratic principles. He frequently ignored public opinion — and the advice of fellow politicians — to pursue his dream of transforming the Turkish state into a modern nation.

The new organization was known as the Free Republican party. Although the party was supportive of many government policies, it opposed the government's role as the chief force in the economy. The members of the new party considered the president an impartial head of state who would not side with either party.

Kemal had created what had seemed to be a safe opposition party — one he could control. What he could not control, however, was the public's response to the new party. Fethi was greeted with wild acclaim everywhere he went. Those who resented the government's antireligious policies, or Kemal and the People's Republican party's total authority, rallied around him. Some of Fethi's speeches were drowned out by the cheers of the crowds, because they were less interested in the details of what he had to say than in simply expressing their enthusiasm for a leader brave enough to stand up to the government.

Kemal's adopted daughters join their father and the leader of the Free Republican party, Ali Fethi (right), in a discussion of the country's new two-party system. This political experiment was short-lived, however — the Free party was disbanded in November 1930 when Fethi's popularity began to rival that of the president himself.

Fethi's tremendous popularity was not only un-expected — it was dangerous as well. As events came to a head, it became clear that Kemal was not an impartial head of state. He openly sided with the People's Republican party against the Free Republican party. Consequently Fethi announced that he was dissolving the party and concluding the experiment in democracy. The Free Republican party had existed for exactly 99 days.

The experience had important benefits, however. "The new party," said Joseph Grew, the American ambassador to Turkey, "had become a clinical thermometer for taking the political temperature of the country and there could be no doubt of the fever which it registered." As a result Mustafa Kemal made a three-month tour of the country to see for himself how things were going for the average Turk. He concluded that the government and the People's Republican party had lost touch with the people they represented. In the following year's parliamen-

Kemal Atatürk addresses parliament in 1935, the year after he took his new surname under the recent law calling for the nationwide adoption of family names. Muslim tradition did not include the use of surnames, a fact that often complicated record keeping and other official business.

tary elections he made a special effort to have new, younger men elected to the Grand National Assembly.

In the mid-1930s Mustafa Kemal announced several more reforms designed to bring Turkey into the mainstream of the western world. These included the adoption of the western Gregorian calendar based on the solar year, to replace the Islamic Hijri calendar, which was determined by lunar cycles. Similarly, Sunday was designated the official weekly day of rest, rather than Friday, the traditional Muslim sabbath. These measures, like Kemal's earlier, more fundamental reforms, were intended to deprive traditional Islam of legitimacy and to emphasize the nonreligious nature of the new Turkey.

Finally Mustafa Kemal presided over yet another reform designed both to sever ties with the past and to westernize Turkey. Late in 1934 he was able to have a law passed calling for all Turks to adopt a family name, or surname. Traditionally, people in Muslim societies were known only by their given names and that of their father (for example, Ahmed, son of Mehmed). This often led to confusion, especially in official records. In addition, many aristocratic families did use family names. Thus the very existence of a family name was a sign of social status and so encouraged snobbery and discrimination. If everyone had a family name, Kemal reasoned, such ugly social distinctions would be harder to preserve, and Turkish society would become more

American Ambassador Joseph Grew was enthusiastic about the changes he saw in the Turkish parliament during the days of the Free Republican party. He commented that "now everyone is full of zest, important points are freely debated . . . a real Parliamentary atmosphere prevails."

open and egalitarian than in the past. In general the law was widely supported.

Kemal personally chose names for some of his closest associates; for example he gave Prime Minister Ismet the name Inönü, the site of the first Turkish military victory in the war with Greece. For Mustafa Kemal himself a special law was passed assigning to him the name of Atatürk, meaning Father Turk. The law specified that no one else could ever use this name. The great national leader dropped his given name of Mustafa because he had come to think of it as too Arabic. From then on he called himself Kemal Atatürk, signing his name simply as "K. Atatürk."

Through much of his life, Atatürk — so strong and seemingly invulnerable in public life — suffered from a variety of illnesses. His service as a young man in primitive regions, such as Libya, had exposed him to malaria, and he was plagued with agonizing bouts of the disease in later years. Often these attacks came at moments of maximum stress — even during the critical Battle of Gallipoli in 1915. His kidneys also gave him a great deal of trouble, resulting in a lengthy stay at a convalescent home in Europe at the end of World War I. Added to these problems were the effects of his irregular life-style. He smoked a great deal and often drank alcohol to excess. He had difficulty sleeping throughout his adult life and often stayed up all night. Sometimes, in fact, he went without sleep for several nights in a row.

Atatürk was a restless and impatient person who was very intolerant of weakness, whether in himself or in others. At the same time he had feelings of immortality — perhaps prompted by such experiences as his narrow escape with a shrapnel wound in the heat of the Battle of Gallipoli. Considering these traits, it is no wonder that Atatürk dismissed early symptoms of serious illness until it was too late for doctors to cure him.

It is said, for example, that during a physical examination the doctor asked him how many cigarettes he smoked per day. "Four packs," Atatürk reportedly answered. Shocked, the doctor ordered

Prime Minister Ismet Inönü had a sometimes stormy relationship with President Atatürk. Nonetheless, he was Atatürk's chosen successor. Despite the fact that he drew criticism for his slow decision making and enthusiasm for Kemal's economy, Inönü proved to be an able national leader.

him to cut his consumption in half. Later an aide asked him why he had lied, since he did not smoke as many packs a day as he had said. "If I had told him the truth," he responded, "he would have cut me down to only one pack a day, and I couldn't stand that!"

Atatürk, who was 57 when he died, may have brought on his own early death because of his personal habits. He might well have lived for many more years if his heavy drinking had not led to cirrhosis of the liver. His last illness was painful. It came on slowly and dragged on over a long time. During most of the last year of his life he often suffered from high fevers and a badly swollen stomach which left him confined to his bed. A highly skilled French physician was at his side during most of this time, but there was little the doctor could do.

Atatürk's illness was well hidden from the public; his death on November 10, 1938, came as a terrible shock. Millions of people mourned as though they had lost their own father. At Istanbul, as his body

BROWN BROTHERS

Although many of his methods were controversial, the founder of the Turkish nation, Kemal Atatürk, is remembered as a champion of progress, western ideals, and, above all, the integrity of the Turkish people.

Atatürk stares past Turkey's national emblem to look out the window of his private train. Although he had seemed almost immortal during his youthful exploits on the battlefield, his last years were marked by illness and extreme physical pain as a lifetime of physical excess began to take its toll.

was borne across the waters of the Bosporus, the funeral vessel was saluted by ships of all the European states, which would soon be at war again. In the middle of the night rural villagers thronged to meet the train that carried his body from Istanbul to its final resting place in Ankara, lighting the way with homemade torches. Without question this great leader had won the deep love of many of his people and the respect of the nations of the world.

Many feared that Atatürk's death just as war in Europe seemed inevitable would leave Turkey rudderless at a crucial time. But they underestimated the soundness of his achievements. Before he died he guaranteed a smooth transition of leadership, arranging for the election of Ismet Inönü, his most trusted adviser and longtime prime minister, as president of the Turkish Republic. Inönü was committed to the preservation and further advancement of Atatürk's reforms. During World War II and after, he proved to be an extremely capable national leader who was able to guide his country through perilous times.

Today Atatürk's body rests beneath a majestic mausoleum on a hill overlooking the heart of the capital city of Ankara, a city he himself built. His deathbed and the room in which he died have been left exactly as they were at his final moment in life. Every year at 9 A.M. on November 10, all Turks stop whatever they are doing and pause for a moment of silent respect for the founder of their nation, "Father Turk."

Atatürk was a determined and in many ways a ruthless person, and he was feared for good reason. He responded to the drastic situation of his nation with drastic — and sometimes violent — measures, but he never resorted to unremitting barbarity as other national leaders have when given total governmental authority. Although he certainly had a great love of power, he used it primarily to further his vision of the new Turkey.

Atatürk's achievements are undeniable. He took a defeated people and inspired them with his enthusiasm and bold ideas. He led the Turkish people confidently and instilled them with hope and pride.

> *Look. A piece of history is passing away.*
> —HASSAN RIZA
> Atatürk's secretary, at his deathbed

Thousands of Turks gather at Atatürk's mausoleum, which overlooks the nation's capital. Each year, on the November 10 anniversary of his death, the Turkish people observe a moment of silence in remembrance of their leader.

With this new spirit as building material, he enacted a dramatic and radical series of reforms that turned the attention of the country from the past to the future. He built the institutions necessary to make the new spirit solid and enduring. The modern Republic of Turkey stands in place of a corrupt and decaying Ottoman Empire, a lasting reminder of what courageous leadership can accomplish.

Kemal Atatürk always looked to the future. That is the reason he saw Turkish youth as his greatest legacy. His charge to them is frequently quoted in Turkey even today: ". . . O Turkish child of future generations, it is your duty to save the independence of the Turkish Republic. The strength that you will need for this is mighty in the noble blood which flows in your veins."

Further Reading

Edib, Halide. *The Turkish Ordeal.* New York: Century, 1928.

Kazancigil, Ali, and Ergun Ozbudun. *Atatürk: Founder of a Modern State.* Hamden, CT: Archon Books, 1981.

Kinross, Lord. *Atatürk: A Biography of Mustafa Kemal, Father of Modern Turkey.* New York: Morrow, 1965.

Landau, Jacob M., ed. *Atatürk and the Modernization of Turkey.* Boulder: Westview Press, 1984.

Lewis, Bernard. *The Emergence of Modern Turkey.* London: Oxford University Press, 1968.

Tachau, Frank. *Turkey: The Politics of Authority, Democracy, and Development.* New York: Praeger, 1984.

Volkan, Vamik D., and Norman Itzkowitz. *The Immortal Atatürk: A Psychobiography.* Chicago: University of Chicago Press, 1984.

Chronology

1881	Born Mustafa in Salonika (now part of Greece)
1893	Enters Salonika's Military Secondary School, where he receives the name Kemal
1905	Graduates from the Staff College; commissioned as a captain
July 24, 1908	Young Turk Revolution forces Sultan Abdülhamid to restore the constitution and reconvene parliament
1913–14	Kemal serves as military attaché at the Ottoman embassy in Sofia, Bulgaria
1914	Ottoman Empire enters World War I on the side of the Central Powers
April–Dec. 1915	Kemal leads the successful defense of the Gallipoli peninsula
Oct. 30, 1918	Armistice of Mudros ends war for the Ottoman Empire
1919	Kemal appointed inspector general and assigned to Samsun; organizes resistance to Greek occupation of Turkish territory
April 23, 1920	Dissolved parliament reconvenes at Angora as the Grand National Assembly; Kemal is elected president of the assembly
Sept. 9, 1922	Greek troops driven from Asia Minor by Kemal's nationalist army
Nov. 1, 1922	Grand National Assembly votes to abolish the sultanate
July 24, 1923	The Ottoman Empire and the Allies sign the Treaty of Lausanne
Oct. 29, 1923	The Ottoman Empire is dissolved; Kemal elected president of the new Republic of Turkey
1925	Kemal cracks down on his political critics, banning the Progressive Republican party and closing down newspapers
Aug. 1930	Authorizes creation of the short-lived Free Republican party
1934	Law requiring the adoption of family names passed; Kemal assumes the name Atatürk (Father Turk)
Nov. 10, 1938	Atatürk dies after a lengthy illness

Index

Frank Tachau is professor of political science at the University of Illinois at Chicago, and chairman of the department. He is also treasurer of the American Research Institute in Turkey. He has published many articles and several books about Turkey and other Middle Eastern subjects, most recently *Turkey: The Politics of Authority, Democracy, and Development.*

Arthur M. Schlesinger, jr., taught history at Harvard for many years and is currently Albert Schweitzer Professor of the Humanities at City University of New York. He is the author of numerous highly praised works in American history and has twice been awarded the Pulitzer Prize. He served in the White House as special assistant to Presidents Kennedy and Johnson.

10524